Live By Design, Not Default

A Doctor's Guide to Health, Wealth, and Purpose

Nicole Alexander-Spencer, MD.

Published by Writers of the West

I dedicate this book to my family.

To my mother, whose unconditional love shaped the person I am today.

To my father, whose pride I have always hoped to earn and honor.

To my husband, who lovingly supports all of my wild ideas and new adventures.

And to my children, into whose lives I have poured my heart, to give them a strong foundation for their growing mind, body, and soul, so they may live with purpose, passion, and a desire to contribute to a better world.

Acknowledgments

This book is the result of the support, belief, and encouragement of many incredible people.

Thank you to my editors for helping me transform my thoughts into words on paper and for guiding this project with care and clarity.

I am deeply grateful to my dance teacher at SDSCPA, Donald Robinson, for believing in me and nurturing confidence, discipline, and self-expression that continue to shape who I am today.

To my close friends, Lilia, Ottilie, Jenn, Kari, and Fermina, Lynel, Omer, DJ, Deonza, Bernie, Roberta, Glenna & Marcia, thank you for being a sounding board, offering honest feedback, and providing unwavering support throughout this journey.

To my medical school crew, Thelma, Tiffany, and Sophie, thank you for the camaraderie, encouragement, and shared experiences that carried us through challenging and transformative years.

To my patients, thank you for entrusting me with your stories and allowing me into your most intimate and vulnerable moments. It is an honor to be your physician, and I care for each of you deeply. Your experiences have profoundly shaped the heart of this book.

I am grateful to my health team at Life Design, Megan, Caroline, Michelle, and Jada, whose dedication and collaboration contribute to patient wellness every single week.

Thank you to the University of Arizona faculty, staff, and my classmates for creating such a meaningful Integrative Fellowship and for supporting the expansion of my medical knowledge and approach to whole-person care.

I am thankful to UCLA for sparking my excitement for higher education and providing a wonderful undergraduate experience.

And finally, thank you to Howard University College of Medicine for giving me the opportunity to make my dream of becoming a physician a reality. The nurturing environment and sense of community shaped me in ways that will forever influence how I practice medicine and care for others.

Table of Contents

Part 1
Cultivating Your Inner World

Chapter 1: The Power of Presence and Intention

Start Here, Start Now

"Good morning God, good morning beautiful, it's going to be a great day."

How would it feel to wake up with more energy? To move through your days with purpose instead of merely surviving them? To design a life that feels intentional rather than chaotic?

One morning, after reading yet another popular self-help book written by an influencer, I woke up with a revelation. I wanted to write a book that summarized simple, actionable steps to lead a balanced, peaceful, and intentional life; a life designed with purpose. Why? Because I had been reading self-help books voraciously, believing I needed constant fixing. I hated my ignorance about almost everything: money, fashion, relationships. I had devoured everything from finance guides to wellness books, cookbooks to spiritual texts, always searching for the missing piece.

But the real catalyst came from my profession. As a physician, I found myself repeating the same recommendations twenty times a day: eat better, lose weight, exercise more, manage your stress. I thought, "People need to know this information; a book would be so much more efficient."

During my integrative medicine training under Dr. Andrew Weil, I learned a fundamental truth: the mind, body, and spirit are interconnected. When one element is off, it affects the others. If your mind is anxious, it interferes with sleep. Chronic sleep deprivation leads to disease because your body doesn't have time to repair itself. I realized that true wellness isn't just about treating symptoms, it's about creating a foundation for thriving.

The Ship Without a Compass

After investing thirteen years in higher education to reach my career, I found myself unable to help certain patients with chronic, common health issues like headaches, constipation, and sleep problems. This frustrated me deeply. I returned to school for a two-year Fellowship in Integrative Medicine at the University of Arizona, but even then, I was living my life by default, like so many people do.

Life was happening to me. I wasn't intentional. I was a ship sailing in open waters without any direction.

My first doctor jobs were miserable. I moved around to different clinics several times in my career, always blaming external circumstances. I finally suffered from burnout, a state I'd later give a TEDx talk about. I had to find my way out of this situation without blaming others. That was really hard because it's so easy to say it's corporate medicine's fault.

Of course, I wanted to run away and live on an island in Hawaii, but that would get boring. I needed to learn what my burnout was teaching me.

I realized I was working too many hours and seeing too many patients per day. The pressure was insane, rushing from patient to patient with only fifteen minutes to see someone, write orders, complete notes, and repeat this cycle ten times daily. I felt worst when I had all three exam rooms full plus a patient on video call, all waiting. I felt terrible making anyone wait.

That's when I decided to design my career and specifically design my schedule. I decreased my hours and transitioned to a four-day work week. I created a clinic culture that was family-like, peaceful and fun with no drama. I took charge by simply writing out what I wanted for myself as a balanced physician so I could show up as my best version for my patients.

I KonMari'd my schedule. I filled it only with things that brought me joy.

What Is Your Why?

Attention grows where energy flows. But first, you need to know your why.

It took me a while to figure this out. Why are we put on this earth? I believe it's to make a positive impact in the world. What are your talents and skills? Don't be selfish, you need to share them.

I think medicine is a calling that allows someone to impact many lives. Being curious and extremely self-motivated are good traits to have in any field.

When I was in middle school, I performed in a play that sparked something inside me. The director was a well-respected dance teacher at San Diego Performing and Creative Arts school. I wanted to go to that school and take dance with him. I was determined.

I begged my mom to enroll me. The school had a waitlist, but I was relentless at thirteen. I pleaded, I called them every day, I made myself impossible to ignore. I eventually got into that school. I became a triple threat, singer (not the best), dancer, and actor. Instead of PE, we had dance. I loved learning and got good grades. Best of all, my mom saved thousands of dollars on private dance, singing, and acting lessons.

This is an example of intention and goal-setting in action. I wanted something, and I figured out how to make it happen. Life works the same way. Whether you want a better body, nicer car, great career, beautiful relationship, bigger house, more money, or weight loss, you can achieve any of these goals. It takes focus, action, and intention.

Keep reading.

Morning Rituals: Setting Your Intentional Foundation

How do you wake up? Alarm clock, then immediately pick up your phone? I'm not going to lie, I still do that sometimes. But let me invite you to another way of being. Just try it.

When you wake up, try a five-minute guided meditation using one of the many apps available. My favorite is Insight Timer. It sets the tone for the entire day. I usually pick one focused on gratitude because when you're grateful, it's hard to be mad, worried, or angry.

Mornings are peaceful, especially if you're an early riser. You can start your day with fewer distractions. Use the morning to stretch, read, pray, or work out. If you have to rush to work or drop off kids, condense your morning ritual, but don't eliminate it.

The Power of Mantras

Have you noticed that while you're taking a shower, your brain just runs wild? It jumps from "this water is hot" to your to-do list, to what you're going to eat, to "I hate work." You need to insert mantras here.

Try these: "Good morning God, good morning beautiful, it's going to be a great day", embracing gratitude and positivity. Set daily intentions and express gratitude: "I love my job. I am so grateful to be working. I am grateful for the sun and the beautiful California weather."

Create your own: "I am grateful for..."

Mindful Movement and Affirmations

Integrate positive affirmations into daily routines. While washing your face: "I am cleaning my face." While brushing your teeth: "I am brushing my teeth." During showers: "I am cleaning my body." During meals: "I am drinking my tea. I am eating my soup, and it tastes delicious."

This is the importance of present-moment awareness throughout the day.

The Science of Meditation: Your Stress-Reduction Toolkit

Meditation is an effective tool for reducing stress through both psychological and physiological mechanisms, helping you better manage your reaction to stressors while cultivating greater calm.

Psychological Benefits

Present-Moment Awareness: Many sources of stress come from dwelling on past regrets or worrying about future anxieties. Meditation, particularly mindfulness meditation, trains your attention to focus on the present moment. By observing your thoughts and feelings without judgment, you become less likely to get caught up in the stream of thoughts that often crowds the mind and causes stress.

Enhanced Emotional Regulation: Meditation helps create space between a stressful thought or event and your reaction to it. Instead of reacting automatically, you learn to observe your emotions and choose a more balanced response, reducing emotional reactivity.

Reduced Rumination: Meditation can break the cycle of repeatedly thinking about negative thoughts or experiences. By gently redirecting your attention back to a focal point like your breath, you train your mind to disengage from unproductive thought patterns.

Physiological Benefits

Research using neuroimaging shows that regular meditation can lead to brain changes. It can decrease the size and activity of the amygdala, the brain's "fight-or-flight" center responsible for stress response. Simultaneously, it can increase the size of the prefrontal cortex, the area associated with attention, decision-making, and emotional regulation.

Meditation also reduces stress hormones like cortisol. Chronic high cortisol levels can impair the immune system and contribute to various health problems. By lowering these levels, meditation helps the body repair itself and reduces the physical damage of chronic stress.

Simple Techniques to Start

Apps: Insight Timer is one of my favorite meditation apps, offering guided sessions for every experience level.

4-7-8 Breathing: This short breathing technique helps during stressful moments. I use it during hectic clinic days. Inhale for 4 counts, hold for 7, exhale for 8.

Start Small: Meditation can seem difficult at first, but just start. Try a three-minute meditation, then build to ten minutes. I try to start and end my day with meditation. If my morning is rushed, sometimes I can only manage three minutes. If you can't find time to meditate, you're moving too fast and need to slow down.

The Art of Slowing Down

Slowing down was a difficult concept for me. My motto used to be "fill up the day and be productive." I had no buffer time and was constantly late to everything. I was addicted to productivity, it made me happy. The faster I went, the more I accomplished, but the more stressed I became.

Piling tasks on top of more tasks, multitasking constantly, there's a time and place for productivity, but constant productivity leads to burnout. It's not sustainable.

I realized I'm most productive Monday mornings from 8 AM to 5 PM, probably because after a restful, non-working weekend, I'm ready to start my week. I learned to love my downtime, which includes sleeping in, slow mornings, and Korean spa days. I was floored when I observed people at the spa just laying in the common room, taking naps, and doing nothing in the middle of the day. We need that.

Challenge: Schedule downtime this week. I have Thursdays off and schedule my downtime then. I love having a weekday off so I can handle banking, doctor appointments, or shop at Costco without being hit by shopping carts.

What's your favorite downtime? Schedule it within the next month. Ideas include lunch with friends, walks in nature, sitting at the park, reading at a bookstore, drawing, visiting bodies of water like oceans or lakes, sitting by the pool. No phones, please!

Building Your Spiritual Practice

I love having a spiritual practice. My husband and I pray most mornings. My prayer is usually the same: starting with gratitude for being alive and living where we live, gratitude for my work, prayers for guidance and wisdom, protection and love for my family and friends, and guidance for current issues.

The Vacation Prescription

I hope you've taken a vacation this year. If not, you need to. I had a patient who hadn't taken a proper vacation in over four years. She came to see me for stress, depression, and anxiety. I immediately took her off work, referred her for therapy, and told her to plan a vacation.

She was a corporate professional with no children, no spouse, and no boundaries. She worked day and night, and it was taking a toll on her mental and physical health. She was experiencing memory problems and undergoing evaluation with a neurologist, but I was certain chronic work stress was contributing to her physical symptoms.

Designing Your Calendar

Figure out your prime productive time and schedule breaks accordingly. Write out your daily schedule for the week. Organize everything in your calendar, on your phone or written, including time for commuting, exercise, lunch, meals with friends and family, sleep, downtime, and playtime.

During your commute, you have an opportunity to "fill the space" with audio books, morning affirmations, or uplifting music.

The Non-Negotiable: Sleep

Don't skimp on sleep, minimum seven hours. Make sure your bedroom is for sex and sleep only, and keep it cool, quiet, and dark. Invest in the best mattress you can afford.

Sleep hygiene is crucial: wind down properly, avoid screens two hours before bed, and don't use drugs or alcohol as sleep aids.

My bedroom is like a cocoon. No animals or kids allowed! For every additional heartbeat in your room, sleep quality decreases by 45 minutes.

Feed Your Soul with Hobbies

Hobbies nourish your soul. My hobby right now is writing this book. If I weren't writing during this block of time before bed, I'd be wasting time scrolling through social media, falling down Facebook rabbit holes.

My hobbies include being in nature, exercising, going to the beach, reading, and traveling. What are yours? Do you like cooking, gardening, drawing? What are you best at? What activity makes you lose track of time?

Give this serious thought. If you're not regularly engaging in your hobbies, why not? Make space, insert time here for your hobbies. You'll be happier.

Stress Management: "It's Not the Issue, It's How You Deal with the Issue"

As my University of Santa Monica professors taught me, stress itself isn't the problem, it's how we respond to it. Stress causes reactivity and irritability, but we have more control than we think.

Short-term stress, like taking a test, is healthy. Chronic stress, like being a caregiver to aging parents, being a new mother without help, not getting enough sleep, working night shifts, being with an abusive partner, or working in a toxic environment, is where real damage occurs.

Stress Management Strategies

Pause Before Reacting: Don't make big decisions during emotional times.

Reframe: When someone cuts me off in traffic, instead of getting angry, I reframe it. Maybe they're rushing to the hospital because they're having a baby.

My job is stressful, rushing from patient to patient with only fifteen minutes per person. My stress management involves being intentional, not rushing, observing my mental messages, exercising, getting at least seven hours of sleep, eating a clean diet full of whole foods with protein at every meal, limiting caffeine and alcohol, drinking water, getting weekly massages, stretching, monthly acupuncture and therapy, recharging with friends and family, and asking for help.

A Note to Caregivers and New Mothers

Take care of yourself. I think I suffered from postpartum depression but didn't realize the huge hormonal changes would take such a toll on my brain, combined with lack of sleep. Often we sacrifice our needs while pouring into another soul or new child.

No one caught my sadness, not even my gynecologist during my postpartum check. I was tearful and felt isolated. I had this wonderful new baby, but these were big changes for me. I was used to busy, hectic work schedules, and now I had to care for this little one.

Mother support groups saved my life. Mommy-and-me groups and caregiver groups are available in most communities. Ask for referrals from trusted sources like doctors. I joined as many as I could to find my community. I met one of my dearest friends this way, our kids are just three days apart. We've been through all the ups and downs of motherhood together: Halloweens, birthdays, teen years, retreats.

Understanding Mental Health

The World Health Organization estimates that globally, 5% of people are depressed, 280 million people. In the US, the National Institute of Health reported in 2021 that 21 million adults, or 8.3% of the US adult population, experience depression. It's 50% more common in women, with higher rates in young adults aged 18-25.

Depression is complex and multifactorial, involving:

Biological factors: Brain chemistry regulating mood, sleep, and appetite. Imbalances in serotonin, dopamine, and norepinephrine contribute to depression.

Genetics: Having a close relative with depression increases your risk, though it's not a guarantee.

Hormones: Postpartum depression, menopause, and thyroid issues can trigger depression.

Physical health: Chronic diseases like heart disease, diabetes, and chronic pain are strongly associated with depression.

Psychological factors: Negative thinking patterns, low self-esteem, and being overly self-critical contribute to depression.

Trauma and stress: Stressful life events like death of a loved one, job loss, major life changes, or breakups can trigger depression. Early life trauma, including parental divorce or abuse, also increases risk.

Social and environmental factors: Lower income, discrimination, racism, social inequity, loneliness, and lack of social support networks are significant risk factors.

Lifestyle factors: Sedentary behavior, sleep deprivation, and poor nutrition contribute to depression.

Depression is not a sign of weakness. You can't just "snap out of it." It's a medical condition requiring a holistic approach, often a combination of therapy, medication, and lifestyle changes.

You may need a therapist. There's no shame in seeking help.

Your Starting Point: One Small Change

What's one small change you can make today?

Consider starting a seven-day kickstart: meditate for five minutes, call a therapist, prioritize sleep, take a walk, drink more water, or practice gratitude.

The journey of a thousand miles begins with a single step. You don't have to transform your entire life overnight. You just need to start here, start now, with intention.

Your designed life is waiting for you. The question is: are you ready to take the first step?

In the next chapter, we'll explore how to nourish your body with intentional nutrition, turning food into medicine and fuel for your designed life.

Reflection Questions for Chapter 1

1. What is your "why"? What positive impact do you want to make in the world?
2. Describe your current morning routine. What one element could you add to make it more intentional?
3. What does your ideal "slow down" time look like? When will you schedule it this week?

4. What stress management technique resonates most with you? How will you implement it?
5. If you could change one thing about your relationship with sleep, what would it be?

Chapter 1 Action Items

This Week:

- Choose one morning ritual to implement (meditation, gratitude, mindful movement)
- Schedule 30 minutes of downtime
- Practice the 4-7-8 breathing technique during one stressful moment

This Month:

- Establish a consistent sleep schedule with a 7-hour minimum
- Identify and begin one hobby that feeds your soul
- Consider whether you need professional support for mental health

Start Today: Choose the smallest possible action from this chapter and do it right now. Your future self will thank you.

Part 2: Nourishing Your Body

Chapter 2: Nourishing Your Body – Intentional Nutrition

"Let food be thy medicine and medicine be thy food." - Hippocrates

The Foundation of Wellness Starts on Your Plate

After investing thirteen years in medical training, I faced a humbling reality: I couldn't help many of my patients with their most common complaints. Chronic headaches that wouldn't respond to medication. Persistent constipation. Unrelenting fatigue. Sleep problems that defied conventional treatment.

The answer, I discovered during my integrative medicine fellowship, had been sitting in front of me all along. It was on their plates three times a day.

During my training under Dr. Andrew Weil at the University of Arizona, I learned a fundamental principle that changed how I practice medicine: food is not just fuel. Food is information. Every bite you take sends signals to your genes, influences your hormones, affects your brain chemistry, and either promotes inflammation or fights it.

The anti-inflammatory diet I learned during that fellowship became the cornerstone of how I help my patients heal. Not with prescriptions alone, but with grocery lists. Not just with medication, but with meal plans.

I repeat this message twenty times a day in my practice, which is one reason I'm writing this book. People need to understand that the most powerful pharmacy isn't at CVS or Walgreens, it's in your kitchen.

What Is an Anti-Inflammatory Diet?

The anti-inflammatory diet emphasizes foods that reduce chronic inflammation in your body. Why does this matter? Because chronic inflammation is the root cause of nearly every disease we face: arthritis, heart disease, diabetes, cancer, Alzheimer's, and autoimmune conditions.

Think of inflammation as your body's fire alarm system. Acute inflammation, like when you sprain your ankle and it swells, is healthy and protective. Chronic inflammation is like a fire alarm that never stops ringing. It exhausts your system and damages healthy tissue over time.

The foods we eat either fan the flames of inflammation or help extinguish them.

When I explain this to patients, I keep it simple: if it's colorful, whole, and recognizable as something that grew from the earth or swam in the ocean, it's probably anti-inflammatory. If it comes in a package with more than five ingredients, many of which you can't pronounce, it's probably inflammatory.

The Foods That Heal

Colorful Fruits and Vegetables

The deeper the color, the more powerful the antioxidants. Blueberries are among my favorites, packed with compounds that combat oxidative stress, a major driver of inflammation. I tell patients to "eat the rainbow": dark leafy greens like spinach and kale, orange sweet potatoes, red bell peppers, purple cabbage, yellow squash.

Cruciferous vegetables, broccoli, cauliflower, Brussels sprouts, contain compounds that support your body's natural detoxification processes. I personally load my dinner plate with sautéed vegetables seasoned with turmeric and black pepper. The combination isn't just delicious; the pepper enhances turmeric's anti-inflammatory properties by up to 2,000 percent.

Healthy Fats

This is where people get confused. "Doctor, isn't fat bad for me?" they ask.

Not all fats are created equal. Healthy fats are essential for brain function, hormone production, and reducing inflammation.

Extra virgin olive oil is the gold standard. I use it almost exclusively in my kitchen, drizzled over salads or used for low to medium-heat cooking. For higher heat, coconut oil works well, though it contains saturated fat and should be used in moderation.

Nuts and seeds, almonds, walnuts, chia seeds, flaxseeds, provide both healthy fats and fiber. A handful of nuts makes an excellent snack that stabilizes blood sugar instead of spiking it.

Fatty fish like salmon, mackerel, and sardines contain omega-3 fatty acids that are profoundly anti-inflammatory. I aim for fatty fish twice a week. When patients tell me they don't like fish, I suggest they try different preparations or consider a high-quality fish oil supplement.

Whole Grains

Notice I said whole grains, not refined grains. Brown rice maintains its nutrient-rich bran and germ layer, while white rice has been stripped of these components during processing. The difference is significant: brown rice provides fiber that slows digestion and prevents blood sugar spikes. White rice breaks down rapidly, causing inflammation.

Oatmeal, quinoa, and farro are excellent whole grain options. If you're making roti, the Indian flatbread, from whole wheat flour and water, that's better than white bread because it's less processed, contains no yeast, and uses whole grain flour. But even roti should be eaten in moderation as a condiment-sized portion rather than the main event.

Herbs and Spices

This is where cooking becomes medicine. Turmeric, ginger, garlic, cinnamon, and cayenne pepper all possess anti-inflammatory properties. I season almost everything I cook with at least two or three of these.

My morning routine includes a golden milk latte: warm almond milk with turmeric, ginger, cinnamon, and a touch of honey. It's become as essential to me as my meditation practice.

Legumes

Beans, lentils, and chickpeas provide both fiber and plant-based protein. They're inexpensive, versatile, and extraordinarily good for you. Mediterranean and Middle Eastern cuisines center around legumes for good reason, hummus made with chickpeas, olive oil, tahini, and lemon juice contains fewer than five ingredients and checks all the anti-inflammatory boxes.

When I traveled to Turkey, my neighbor taught me that adding a touch of vinegar to hummus extends its freshness. Simple wisdom that honors whole foods.

The Foods That Harm

Stay Away From the White Stuff

I tell every patient: avoid white bread, white rice, white pasta, and white sugar. These refined carbohydrates have been stripped of their nutrients and fiber. They spike your blood sugar, trigger insulin release, promote fat storage, and create inflammation.

Refined carbohydrates also feed the harmful bacteria in your gut, disrupting the delicate balance of your microbiome. More on that shortly.

Ultra-Processed Foods

Here's my rule of thumb: if a packaged food has more than five ingredients, or ingredients with multiple syllables you can't pronounce, it's ultra-processed.

Fast food. Packaged snacks. Frozen dinners. Processed meats like hot dogs, sausages, and deli meats. These contain preservatives, additives, trans fats, and sodium levels that promote inflammation and are linked to cancer and heart disease.

When patients cook bacon and see all that fat pooling in the pan, I remind them: that fat doesn't just disappear after you eat it. It's coating your arteries, contributing to heart disease.

Sugar and Sugary Drinks

This is perhaps the most damaging category. Americans are drinking their calories through sodas, sweetened coffees, energy drinks, and fruit juices. A single soda contains roughly 200 calories of pure sugar, no nutrients, just inflammation.

If you're consuming 1,600 calories a day to maintain a healthy weight, drinking three sodas means you've consumed nearly 40 percent of your daily calories from sugar water. It's one reason we're facing an obesity epidemic.

Diet sodas aren't the solution. Artificial sweeteners like aspartame and sucralose come with their own health concerns, including possible cancer risk and disruption of gut bacteria. When I see patients ordering a massive meal with a Diet Coke, I gently point out the contradiction. That artificial sweetener isn't saving you from the inflammatory load of processed food.

The Alcohol Question

Patients frequently ask about alcohol. Here's what the research shows: if you don't drink, don't start. If you do drink, moderation is key.

Red wine contains polyphenols, the anti-inflammatory compounds found in grape skins. A glass with dinner may offer some benefit. However, alcohol is still a toxin your liver must process. It's calorie-dense at 7 calories per gram, promotes weight gain, and can become addictive.

For women, no more than seven drinks per week. For men, no more than fourteen. Beyond that, you're causing more harm than any potential benefit.

I have a friend who swears beer "filters his kidneys." I had to break the difficult news: alcohol is a toxin that stresses your kidneys and liver, not helps them. The calories in beer contribute significantly to weight gain, what we call a "beer belly" is inflammation and fat storage.

Your Gut: The Second Brain

One of the most exciting areas of research in medicine right now is the gut microbiome, the community of trillions of bacteria, viruses, and fungi living in your digestive tract.

We're born with our first microbiome colonization during vaginal delivery, when we're exposed to our mother's bacteria. Breastfeeding continues to seed our gut with beneficial organisms. Throughout life, our microbiome remains in constant flux, influenced by what we eat, medications we take, stress levels, and environmental exposures.

Here's what fascinates me: people in America have far less microbial diversity than people living in traditional villages in Africa. Our Western diet, high in processed foods and low in fiber, has decimated our gut ecosystems. We're now discovering links between poor gut health and depression, anxiety, autism, obesity, diabetes, and even dementia.

The gut produces neurotransmitters like serotonin that affect mood and mental health. There's a gut-brain axis, a direct communication highway between your digestive system and your mind. This is why addressing depression sometimes requires fixing the gut, not just prescribing antidepressants.

Rebuilding Your Microbiome

Fermented foods are your allies: kimchi, sauerkraut, kombucha, kefir, and naturally fermented pickles. These contain beneficial bacteria that colonize your gut.

Fiber feeds the good bacteria. Aim for at least 30 grams daily from vegetables, fruits, whole grains, and legumes.

Probiotics, either from supplements or fermented foods, introduce beneficial organisms. I recommend probiotics especially after antibiotic use, which kills both harmful and helpful bacteria indiscriminately.

Avoid antibiotics unless truly necessary. I'm mindful about prescribing them because they disrupt the microbiome for months afterward.

There was a remarkable study involving rats, one thin, one obese. Researchers transferred gut bacteria from the thin rat into the obese rat through fecal transplant. The obese rat began losing weight. The implications are staggering: our gut bacteria may influence our ability to maintain a healthy weight.

While we're not doing routine fecal transplants for obesity yet, this research underscores how profoundly food choices affect the microscopic ecosystem within us.

Building Your Anti-Inflammatory Plate

What does a healthy meal actually look like?

Breakfast: Scrambled eggs cooked with turmeric and black pepper, served with avocado and mixed berries. You're getting protein, healthy fat, and antioxidants. No refined carbs, no sugar crash.

Lunch: A large salad with mixed greens, grilled chicken or salmon, olive oil and lemon dressing, topped with walnuts and colorful vegetables. Add a side of lentil soup if you're particularly hungry.

Dinner: Baked salmon with roasted sweet potato and sautéed spinach seasoned with garlic and ginger. The sweet potato provides complex carbs; the salmon offers omega-3s; the spinach delivers vitamins and minerals.

Notice what's missing? Bread. Pasta. Rice. These aren't forbidden forever, but they shouldn't be the foundation of every meal. When you do eat grains, choose brown rice, quinoa, or steel-cut oats.

The Hydration Equation

Your body is approximately 60 percent water. Every cellular process requires adequate hydration. Yet most Americans are chronically dehydrated, mistaking thirst for hunger and reaching for snacks instead of water.

The formula is simple: drink roughly half your body weight in ounces of water daily. If you weigh 160 pounds, that's 80 ounces, about ten cups or 2.4 liters.

Your urine should be pale yellow, not dark. Dark yellow signals dehydration.

Coffee and tea count toward hydration, but be mindful. One cup of coffee in the morning is fine for most people. I personally can't tolerate caffeine, it makes me anxious and jittery. My daughter has the same sensitivity.

If you're drinking six or seven cups daily, you're chasing the caffeine high and low, creating dependence. You'll experience withdrawal headaches if you try to quit.

Green tea offers a gentler caffeine option plus powerful antioxidants. I drink it throughout the day, choosing decaffeinated varieties when I'm sensitive to stimulation.

Don't Drink Your Calories

This principle is worth repeating. Liquid calories don't trigger satiety the way solid food does. You can drink 500 calories and still feel hungry an hour later.

Starbucks drinks often contain ten or more ingredients, sugar, artificial flavors, preservatives. What started as coffee becomes a 400-calorie dessert.

If you drink coffee, keep it simple: black, or with minimal cream. Skip the flavored syrups and whipped cream.

The Sweetener Dilemma

Sugar is refined, inflammatory, and addictive. But what about alternatives?

Natural options:

- **Honey** and **maple syrup** are less processed but still high in calories and should be used sparingly
- **Stevia** is plant-based, zero-calorie, and doesn't spike blood sugar, a reasonable option in moderation

- **Monk fruit** is another natural, low-calorie sweetener

Avoid:

- **Aspartame, sucralose, and saccharin**, artificial sweeteners linked to gut microbiome disruption and possible health risks
- **Sugar alcohols like xylitol**, can cause digestive distress

When making smoothies, I sweeten with dates rather than sugar. Dates provide natural sweetness plus fiber and minerals.

The goal isn't to replace sugar gram-for-gram with alternatives. The goal is to retrain your palate to appreciate foods that aren't aggressively sweet.

Eating Regularly: The Three-Meal Foundation

Don't skip meals, especially breakfast. When you skip breakfast, you arrive at lunch ravenous and overeat. Or you slow your metabolism, signaling to your body that food is scarce and it should conserve energy by storing fat.

Eat breakfast between 7-9 AM, lunch between 12-1 PM, and dinner between 5-7 PM. This regular schedule stabilizes blood sugar and prevents the energy crashes that lead to poor food choices.

The Snacking Trap

Healthy snacks can bridge meals if you're genuinely hungry: carrot sticks with hummus, a handful of almonds, an apple with almond butter. But most people snack on crackers, chips, cookies, processed foods that spike insulin and promote weight gain.

If you're eating balanced meals with adequate protein, healthy fat, and fiber, you shouldn't need constant snacking. Hunger between meals often signals dehydration, boredom, or emotional eating rather than true physical hunger.

Meal Planning: Your Secret Weapon

The patients who succeed with dietary changes are the ones who plan ahead. When you wait until you're starving to decide what to eat, you'll grab whatever is fastest, usually something processed and unhealthy.

My weekly routine:

- **Sunday afternoon:** I plan meals for the week and create a shopping list
- **Sunday evening:** I prep vegetables, cook proteins in bulk, make a large pot of soup
- **Throughout the week:** I assemble meals quickly from prepped ingredients

I keep hard-boiled eggs in the refrigerator for quick protein. I wash and chop vegetables immediately after grocery shopping so they're ready to cook. I batch-cook chicken breast or salmon to use in multiple meals.

This isn't about spending hours in the kitchen daily. It's about spending two hours once weekly to set yourself up for success.

The Eating Out Challenge

Restaurant meals are typically higher in sodium, sugar, and unhealthy fats than home-cooked food. Portions are enormous, often two or three servings presented as one meal.

When dining out:

- **Ask for dressings and sauces on the side**
- **Request vegetables instead of fries**
- **Order grilled or baked proteins, not fried**
- **Eat half and take the rest home**
- **Skip the bread basket**

I'm not suggesting you never enjoy restaurant meals. I'm suggesting you be intentional about them rather than making them your default.

The Organic Question

Patients frequently ask whether organic food is worth the cost. Here's my stance: anything without a peel should be organic.

Strawberries, blueberries, spinach, kale, these absorb pesticides that you can't wash off. Pesticide exposure is linked to hormone disruption, neurological problems, and cancer risk.

The Environmental Working Group publishes an annual "Dirty Dozen" list of produce highest in pesticide residue. Prioritize buying those items organic.

Produce with thick peels, bananas, avocados, oranges, can be conventional since you're not eating the exterior.

Organic isn't just about what's sprayed on plants. It's about soil quality. Organic farming practices build healthier soil with more diverse microorganisms, which translates to more nutrient-dense food.

Yes, organic costs more. But it's an investment in your health. The money you save buying cheap, processed food will eventually be spent on medical bills treating diet-related diseases.

My Kitchen Essentials

Cooking oils: Extra virgin olive oil (EVOO) for most cooking, coconut oil for high heat

Pantry staples: Brown rice, quinoa, steel-cut oats, canned beans, canned tomatoes, vegetable broth

Spices: Turmeric, black pepper, cumin, cinnamon, garlic powder, ginger

Freezer items: Wild-caught salmon, organic berries, frozen vegetables for convenience

Fresh always: Leafy greens, colorful vegetables, avocados, lemons, garlic, ginger root

Proteins: Eggs, chicken breast, fatty fish, occasional grass-fed beef

I don't keep processed foods in my house. If it's there, I'll eat it. The best way to avoid temptation is to not bring it through your door.

One Patient's Transformation

I had a patient, let's call her Maria, who came to me weighing 240 pounds with Type 2 diabetes, high blood pressure, and high cholesterol. She was on five medications and felt exhausted constantly.

I didn't immediately add more medications. I asked about her diet.

She drank four sodas daily. She ate fast food five times a week. She never cooked. Her idea of vegetables was the lettuce on her burger.

We started simply: replace sodas with water. Add one vegetable to dinner. Cook at home twice weekly.

Within three months, she'd lost 25 pounds. Her blood sugar dropped significantly. She had more energy than she'd felt in years.

Within six months, I reduced two of her medications.

Within a year, she was off diabetes medication entirely, maintaining normal blood sugar through diet alone.

This isn't rare. I see variations of this transformation constantly. Food is that powerful.

But What About...?

"I don't have time to cook."

You don't have time *not* to cook. The hours you lose to poor health, doctors appointments, sick days, low energy, far exceed the time spent preparing healthy meals. Start with just two home-cooked meals weekly and build from there.

"Healthy food is expensive."

Beans, rice, eggs, seasonal vegetables, and frozen fish are inexpensive. What's expensive is convenience, pre-made meals, restaurant food, and later, medical bills from diet-related disease.

"My family won't eat healthy food."

Cook one meal. Don't be a short-order cook making separate meals for everyone. Children learn eating habits from parents. If you normalize vegetables, whole grains, and lean proteins, they'll adapt. It may take time, but consistency works.

"I travel constantly for work."

Pack snacks: nuts, protein bars (check ingredients, many are candy bars in disguise), apples. Research restaurants in advance. Most places offer grilled chicken or fish with vegetables. You have more control than you think.

Simple Recipe: Basic Hummus

Since we discussed it during my conversation with Sarah, here's my go-to hummus recipe:

Ingredients:

- 1 can (15 oz) chickpeas, drained and rinsed
- 3 tablespoons extra virgin olive oil
- 2 tablespoons tahini
- 2 tablespoons lemon juice
- 1 clove garlic
- 1/2 teaspoon cumin
- Pinch of salt
- Touch of vinegar (preserves freshness)

Instructions: Blend all ingredients in food processor until smooth. Add water if too thick. Store in airtight container for up to one week.

Six ingredients, five minutes, deeply nutritious.

The Path Forward

I'm not asking you to overhaul your entire diet overnight. Dramatic changes rarely stick. What works is incremental progress: one meal, one day, one week at a time.

This week, focus on one change:

- Replace one soda with water daily
- Add vegetables to dinner three times
- Cook one meal at home you'd usually eat out
- Swap white rice for brown rice

Next week, add another small change.

In three months, you'll look back amazed at how different your plate, and your health, looks.

Your body is remarkable. Given the right nutrients, it knows how to heal. Inflammation decreases. Energy increases. Weight normalizes. Chronic symptoms improve.

You just have to give your body what it's designed to run on: real food.

The most powerful prescription I can write isn't for medication. It's for how you nourish yourself three times a day, every day, for the rest of your life.

Reflection Questions for Chapter 2

1. What is one inflammatory food you eat regularly that you could reduce or eliminate?
2. How many servings of colorful vegetables and fruits do you currently eat daily? What's one way you could increase that number?
3. When you think about meal planning, what barriers come up for you? Are they real constraints or habits that could shift?
4. What's your relationship with water? Are you chronically dehydrated without realizing it?
5. What food from your childhood or culture brings you joy? How could you prepare it in a healthier way that honors both tradition and wellness?

Chapter 2 Action Items

This Week:

- Calculate your daily water needs (body weight divided by 2 = ounces daily)
- Replace one sugary drink with water or green tea
- Add one colorful vegetable to dinner three times this week
- Read labels: identify one "healthy" packaged food in your pantry that's actually ultra-processed

This Month:

- Plan and shop for one week of meals
- Cook at home four times weekly

- Try one new anti-inflammatory recipe
- Replace refined grains (white rice, white bread) with whole grain alternatives
- Increase fiber intake to 30 grams daily through vegetables, fruits, and legumes

This Quarter:

- Establish consistent meal timing (breakfast, lunch, dinner at regular hours)
- Reduce or eliminate processed meats from your diet
- Build a collection of five go-to healthy meals you can prepare easily
- Notice changes in energy, digestion, sleep, and mood as your nutrition improves

Start Today:

Choose the smallest possible action. Drink one glass of water right now. Buy one bunch of leafy greens at your next grocery trip. Swap your afternoon soda for tea.

Small actions, repeated consistently, create transformations you can't yet imagine.

Your journey toward thriving begins with what you put on your plate.

In the next chapter, we'll explore how movement becomes medicine, discovering why exercise isn't just about weight loss, but about building a body that supports your designed life for decades to come.

Chapter 3: Movement as Medicine – Embracing Physical Activity

"Motion is lotion." – Traditional wisdom

Let me be honest with you: exercise is one of those things that almost everyone resists. I see it in my practice daily. Patients nod when I recommend it, then return months later having never started. They sign up for gym memberships in January with New Year's enthusiasm, only to let them gather dust by March. They buy workout clothes, download fitness apps, bookmark YouTube videos, and still never move.

Why? Because exercise requires something many of us struggle with: personal motivation. There's no pill I can prescribe that will make you want to exercise. No injection that creates discipline. No cream that builds the habit of movement into your daily routine.

But here's what I've learned over two decades of practicing medicine: the patients who age most gracefully, who maintain their independence longest, who feel best in their bodies and minds, they're the ones who move regularly.

Exercise isn't just about looking good in a swimsuit or fitting into smaller jeans. It checks boxes across every dimension of wellness: mental health, stress relief, cardiovascular health, weight management, bone density, sleep quality, chronic disease prevention, and longevity.

When one intervention addresses so many health concerns simultaneously, we need to pay attention.

Here's the secret no one tells you: you don't need to wait until you feel motivated to start exercising.

Motivation is fickle. It comes and goes like the weather. If you only exercise when motivated, you'll have gaps, sometimes long ones, in your routine. What you need is to make movement a non-negotiable habit, like brushing your teeth. You don't wait to feel motivated to brush your teeth. You just do it because it's what you do.

The same principle applies to exercise. I tell my patients: "Just do it." Three words. No excuses. Make it a lifestyle.

The official recommendations are straightforward: Thirty minutes of cardiovascular exercise, five days per week. Two days of strength training. That's it. That's the foundation.

Notice I didn't say you need to spend two hours in the gym daily or train for marathons. Thirty minutes, five times weekly, is the bare minimum to maintain health and prevent disease.

Can you do more? Absolutely. Should you do less? Not if you want to optimize your health span, the number of years you live in good health. If you can only manage three days weekly, then those three days need to be longer to compensate. The total weekly minutes matter.

Exercise Versus Movement

I prefer the word "movement" to "exercise" because exercise can feel like a chore, something clinical and unpleasant.

Movement is broader. It encompasses any way you enjoy using your body.

Do you love dancing? Dance. That's exercise.

Prefer hiking in nature? Perfect. That counts.

Enjoy swimming, biking, playing tennis, or taking brisk walks with friends? All excellent forms of cardiovascular activity.

The best exercise is the one you'll actually do consistently.

I've had patients tell me they hate gyms, the fluorescent lighting, the crowds, the mirrors. Fine. Don't go to the gym. Walk outside instead. Put on music and dance in your living room. Find what brings you joy.

The Power of Accountability

One strategy that significantly increases adherence is exercising with someone else. When you commit to meeting a friend for a morning walk, you're far less likely to cancel than if you were just promising yourself you'd go. You don't want to let them down. That external accountability is powerful.

Consider joining group fitness classes, walking clubs, recreational sports leagues, or finding a workout buddy. The social element transforms exercise from solitary suffering into shared experience. My patients who exercise regularly often credit their consistency to the people they exercise with, not just their internal discipline.

Stretching: The Often-Forgotten Component

Before we go further, let me emphasize something that often gets overlooked: **stretching**. It helps prevent injury, maintains flexibility, improves range of motion, and becomes increasingly important as we age. I incorporate stretching into my routine because I've seen too many patients get injured trying to jump into vigorous exercise with tight, inflexible bodies.

Think of stretching as preventive maintenance. You wouldn't drive your car 100,000 miles without changing the oil. Don't ask your body to perform without proper preparation.

Spend five to ten minutes before and after exercise stretching major muscle groups: hamstrings, quadriceps, calves, shoulders, and back.

Exercise as Prescription

When patients come to me with high cholesterol, I don't just reach for the prescription pad. I ask about their exercise routine first.

Exercise lowers blood pressure. Multiple studies show that regular cardiovascular activity reduces both systolic and diastolic blood pressure as effectively as some medications.

Exercise regulates blood sugar. For Type 2 diabetics, muscle contraction during exercise helps cells uptake glucose without requiring as much insulin. This is why I tell diabetic patients that exercise is non-negotiable.

Exercise builds bone density. Weight-bearing activities, walking, jogging, dancing, strength training, signal your body to maintain and build bone mass. This is critical for preventing osteoporosis, especially in postmenopausal women.

Exercise improves mental health. Movement releases endorphins, reduces cortisol, improves sleep, and provides a sense of accomplishment. Many of my patients with mild to moderate depression experience significant improvement with regular exercise.

When one intervention treats multiple conditions, why wouldn't we prioritize it?

Exercise Snacks: Making It Work in Real Life

"I don't have time" is the excuse I hear most frequently.

My response: "You don't have thirty minutes in a twenty-four-hour day?"

If you truly cannot carve out a continuous thirty-minute block, then practice **exercise snacks**, short bursts of activity throughout the day.

Ten minutes before work: a brisk walk around the neighborhood.

Ten minutes during lunch: climb stairs in your office building.

Ten minutes after work: another walk, or a quick bodyweight circuit in your living room.

Those three ten-minute sessions equal your thirty minutes.

The research shows that accumulated activity throughout the day provides similar benefits to one continuous session. Your body doesn't care if you did it all at once or in intervals.

Stop making time an excuse. It's a matter of priority, not availability.

My Personal Routine

People always ask what I personally do for exercise. Here's my honest answer:

I attend Orange Theory Fitness twice weekly because they provide thirty minutes of cardiovascular work plus thirty minutes of strength training in one structured hour-long session. I don't have to think about programming; I just show up and follow the workout.

The other five days, I do a combination of stair climbing and jogging to meet my minimum thirty minutes of cardio.

I'm consistent not because I'm superhuman or exceptionally disciplined, but because I've built systems that remove barriers.

I keep my workout shoes and gym bag packed in my car. When I finish work, I drive straight to the gym before going home. If I go home first, the couch beckons and I'm done for the day. I work out immediately after finishing my clinical hours because that's when it works for me. I'm not a morning person, never have been, never will be. Trying to force myself to exercise at 5 AM would guarantee failure.

Find your optimal time. Honor your body's natural rhythms. Then protect that time fiercely.

Age Matters: Exercise Across the Lifespan

Premenopausal Women

If you're premenopausal, thirty minutes of cardiovascular exercise five days weekly is generally sufficient, though adding strength training improves results. Your body still produces estrogen, which helps maintain muscle mass and bone density. You have more flexibility in your exercise choices.

Menopausal and Postmenopausal Women

This is where things change significantly. Once you enter menopause, you begin losing muscle mass at an accelerated rate due to declining estrogen. This loss continues through postmenopause.

Cardiovascular exercise alone is no longer enough.

You must add **strength training with heavy weights** at least twice weekly to preserve and build muscle. I cannot overstate this: if you weren't lifting weights before menopause, you absolutely must start after. The muscle you lose during and after menopause doesn't come back easily. Prevention is far easier than restoration.

Lifting heavy weights, not just five-pound dumbbells, but weights that challenge your muscles, signals your body to maintain muscle tissue despite hormonal changes.

Strong muscles support your joints, maintain your metabolism, prevent falls, and keep you independent as you age.

Diabetic Patients

I frequently hear the misconception that diabetics shouldn't walk, that they should only do strength training. This is false.

Any exercise is beneficial for diabetics. When muscles contract during activity, whether walking, swimming, or lifting weights, they uptake glucose without requiring as much insulin. This is extraordinarily beneficial for blood sugar control.

The basic recommendation remains: **thirty minutes of cardiovascular exercise, five days weekly**, ideally at a pace that makes you breathless and produces sweat. Not a casual stroll, but brisk walking with purpose.

For walkers, the goal is **10,000 steps daily**. If you achieve this, you've met your exercise quota for the day.

Interval walking is particularly effective: alternate one minute of fast walking (pumping your arms, breathing hard) with one minute of moderate pace. This elevates your heart rate more effectively than steady-state walking.

Pregnant Women

Pregnant women can and should exercise, with some modifications.

If you exercised before pregnancy, you can generally continue the same types of activity, avoiding anything that risks abdominal trauma. I wouldn't recommend skiing when you're eight months pregnant or activities with high fall risk.

Walking is universally safe and beneficial throughout pregnancy.

Regarding heavy weightlifting during pregnancy: I don't recommend it. Your body is undergoing significant changes, and heavy lifting increases risk of injury.

Stick with walking, prenatal yoga, swimming, and light resistance training. Your goal is maintaining fitness, not setting personal records.

After delivery, gradually return to exercise once cleared by your obstetrician, typically around six weeks postpartum for vaginal delivery, longer for cesarean section.

Designing Your Exercise Routine

Let me make this simple.

Minimum requirement: Five days weekly, thirty minutes of cardiovascular exercise that makes you breathe hard and sweat, plus two days of strength training. You can combine cardio and strength training on the same days. That's only five workout days, leaving two days for rest and recovery. If you want to move seven days weekly, I applaud you. Many of my most vital elderly patients walk daily. Movement is a gift, not a burden. But five days is the bare minimum for maintaining health and preventing chronic disease.

Finding Your Optimal Time

There's a certain time of day when your energy peaks. For some, it's early morning. For others, midday. For me, it's immediately after work.

Pay attention to your natural rhythms.

I had a patient who tried for years to become a morning exerciser because that's what all the fitness magazines recommended. She would set her alarm for 5 AM, hit snooze repeatedly, finally drag herself to the gym feeling miserable, have terrible workouts, then quit after a few weeks.

I asked when she naturally felt most energetic. She said lunchtime.

I suggested she exercise during her lunch break, even if it meant eating a quick meal at her desk afterward. She started walking briskly for thirty minutes daily at noon. Six months later, she'd lost fifteen pounds, lowered her blood pressure, and hadn't missed a single workout.

Stop fighting your nature. Work with it.

Some people genuinely do feel best exercising first thing in the morning. If that's you, wonderful. Set out your workout clothes the night before. Put your alarm across the room so you have to get out of bed to turn it off. Drink a glass of water immediately upon waking to activate your system.

But if you're not a morning person, **stop trying to force it**. Find the time that works for your body and your schedule.

Eating and Exercise Timing

A common question: should I eat before or after exercise?

Here's the guideline: **don't exercise on a full stomach**. You'll feel nauseated, sluggish, and uncomfortable.

If you need something before morning exercise, eat something small and easily digestible: a banana, a piece of toast, a few bites of yogurt. Give yourself at least thirty minutes to digest before moving vigorously.

After exercise, eat within an hour to support recovery, ideally including protein to help repair and build muscle.

The idea that you must exercise within fifteen minutes of eating to "burn those calories immediately" is nonsense. Your body burns calories continuously, regardless of when you exercise relative to meals.

Exercise whenever you feel best. Eat when you're hungry. Don't overthink it.

Breaking Through Obstacles

Let me address the most common obstacles I hear:

"I don't have time."

You have time. You're choosing to prioritize other things. I'm not judging, we all make choices based on our values. But be honest with yourself. You have time to scroll social media, watch television, or browse the internet. You could use that time to move your body.

"I can't afford a gym membership."

You don't need one. Walking is free. Bodyweight exercises, pushups, squats, lunges, planks, require no equipment. YouTube offers thousands of free workout videos.

"I don't have anyone to watch my kids."

Many YMCAs and community centers offer childcare. Or exercise with your kids: put them in a stroller and jog. Play tag. Dance together in the living room. When my children were young, I used a double jogging stroller and ran at the park while they enjoyed the ride.

"I'm too tired."

Exercise gives you energy. Yes, you feel tired initially. But regular exercise improves sleep quality, increases daytime energy, and reduces fatigue. You have to push through the first few weeks to experience this benefit.

"I'm too old to start."

You're never too old. I have patients in their seventies and eighties who began regular exercise programs and experienced dramatic improvements in strength, balance, and quality of life. Start where you are. Walk slowly at first. Build gradually. Movement at any pace is better than remaining sedentary.

Motion Is Lotion

As my mother ages, I watch her body stiffen. She moves less, which makes her stiffer, which makes her move even less, a vicious cycle.

Older adults fall not because falling is inevitable with aging, but because they become stiff and weak from inactivity. Their muscles atrophy. Their balance deteriorates. Their bones become brittle.

Motion is lotion. The more you move, the more fluidly your joints function. The less you move, the stiffer you become.

This is true at any age, but becomes critical as we grow older.

If you want to maintain independence, to climb stairs, carry groceries, play with grandchildren, travel, you must keep moving.

The patients I see who are eighty-five and still driving, gardening, and living independently? They're the ones who never stopped moving.

Exercise as Stress Relief

I mentioned earlier that I work out after finishing clinic. There's a reason for that beyond just convenience. Exercise is one of the most effective stress management tools available. My workday involves intense focus, difficult conversations, and emotional labor. I listen to patients' suffering. I deliver bad news. I make high-stakes decisions about medications and treatments. By the end of my clinical day, I'm mentally exhausted but physically wired with residual stress.

Exercise breaks that stress cycle. It metabolizes cortisol, releases endorphins, provides physical outlet for accumulated tension, and creates clear separation between work and home.

I have a sister who runs when she's angry. The madder she gets, the harder and longer she runs. She told me, "I imagine all the things I could have said or done to that person. I run through every scenario. By the time I get home, I'm too exhausted to be angry anymore." That's a healthy coping mechanism.

Some people hit punching bags, boxing provides both exercise and catharsis. Others do aggressive yoga. Find what works for you.

When stress, anger, or anxiety build up, **move your body**. Don't sit with those feelings. Metabolize them through physical activity.

The Blue Zones: Lessons in Longevity

I'm fascinated by the Blue Zones, regions where people routinely live past one hundred years: Sardinia, Italy; Okinawa, Japan; Loma Linda, California; Nicoya Peninsula, Costa Rica; Ikaria, Greece.

Researchers studying these populations identified common factors contributing to longevity:

Plant-based diets with minimal meat consumption.

Natural movement built into daily life, walking hilly terrain, tending gardens, manual labor.

Strong social connections and sense of community.

Clear life purpose that gives meaning to their days.

Notice that formal "exercise" isn't part of the equation. These populations don't go to gyms. They move constantly through daily activities that require physical effort.

Modern life has engineered movement out of our days. We drive instead of walk. We sit at desks instead of working fields. We order groceries online instead of carrying bags home from the market.

We must intentionally reintroduce movement because our environment no longer requires it.

The Blue Zone populations maintain strength, flexibility, and cardiovascular fitness not through deliberate exercise programs, but through movement woven into the fabric of daily life.

You can learn from this: take stairs instead of elevators, walk to nearby destinations instead of driving, do yard work instead of hiring help, play actively with children or grandchildren.

Movement doesn't have to happen in a gym to count.

Functional Fitness: Preparing for Real Life

I prefer exercises that mimic movements you perform in daily life, what we call **functional fitness**. Can you lift a suitcase overhead without injuring yourself? Can you squat down to pick something off the floor and stand back up? Can you carry heavy grocery bags? Can you push open a heavy door? These are functional movements.

Exercises that build functional strength include: squats, lunges, deadlifts, overhead presses, rows, pushups, and planks.

You're training your body for the activities life requires, not just for aesthetic appearance.

As you age, functional fitness determines whether you remain independent or require assistance with basic tasks. I don't want my patients ending up in nursing homes because they can't get off the toilet unassisted. I want them hiking, traveling, and living vigorously into their eighties and nineties. That requires maintaining strength and mobility through regular movement.

The Social Dimension

Exercise doesn't have to be solitary. Some of my happiest, healthiest patients participate in group activities: tennis leagues, hiking clubs, dance classes, cycling groups, water aerobics.

The social connection enhances both enjoyment and adherence. You show up because your friends will be there. You laugh together. You encourage each other. You build community while building fitness.

If you struggle with consistency, join a group. The social pressure, in a positive way, keeps you accountable.

When Exercise Feels Like Punishment

If you view exercise as punishment for having a body or for eating food, something is wrong.

Exercise should feel like celebration, celebrating what your body can do, how it feels to be strong, the gift of movement.

Yes, it's hard sometimes. Yes, you sweat and breathe heavily. But it shouldn't feel like penance.

If exercise feels like torture, you're either:

1. Doing the wrong type of exercise for your preferences
2. Pushing too hard too fast
3. Carrying negative associations about your body that need addressing

Find movement that brings you joy, even if that joy is quiet satisfaction rather than exuberant fun.

I don't love every moment of my workouts. Sometimes I'm tired and would rather skip them. But I always feel better afterward, physically, mentally, emotionally.

That's the payoff I'm chasing: not the workout itself, but how I feel for the twenty-three hours after I finish moving my body.

Starting Where You Are

Maybe you haven't exercised in years. Maybe you've never exercised consistently. Maybe you're significantly overweight or have mobility limitations. *Start where you are.* Don't compare yourself to the fitness influencer on Instagram or your friend who runs marathons. Your journey is your own.

Week one: walk for ten minutes three times. That's it. No judgment about what you "should" be doing.

Week two: walk for fifteen minutes three times.

Week three: walk for twenty minutes four times.

Gradually build duration and frequency. Add intensity when you're ready. Introduce strength training when walking feels manageable. Progress isn't linear. Some weeks you'll do great. Some weeks life will interfere. The key is returning to movement as soon as you can, without guilt or self-flagellation.

Your Action Plan

This week:

- Choose one form of movement you genuinely enjoy.
- Schedule three 30-minute sessions in your calendar. Treat them as unmissable appointments.
- Recruit an accountability partner or join a class.
- Remove barriers: pack your gym bag, lay out workout clothes, identify your optimal exercise time.

This month:

- Build to five 30-minute cardiovascular sessions weekly.
- Add two strength-training sessions.
- Notice how you feel, energy levels, sleep quality, stress levels, mood.

This quarter:

- Establish movement as non-negotiable routine, like brushing your teeth.
- Explore new activities to maintain interest and challenge different muscle groups.
- Celebrate progress: maybe you can walk farther without getting winded, lift heavier weights, or fit into clothes that were tight before.

***

Movement is medicine.

It prevents disease. It extends lifespan. It improves quality of life. It enhances mental health. It's free or low-cost. It has no dangerous side effects.

If I could bottle exercise as a prescription, it would be the most powerful drug in my pharmacy.

But I can't prescribe it. You have to choose it.

Thirty minutes, five days weekly. That's the minimum investment in your future self, the self who wants to travel, play with grandchildren, live independently, and thrive rather than merely survive.

You don't need to be perfect. You just need to be consistent.

Your body is designed to move. Honor that design.

The patients who embrace movement are the ones who come back to me years later, grateful that they started when they did. They tell me it changed their lives, their health, their confidence, their vitality.

They're not superhuman. They're just consistent.

That can be you.

Movement is a choice you make every single day.

What will you choose?

***

In the next chapter, we'll explore the often-overlooked pillar of health: rest, recovery, and renewal, learning why doing nothing is sometimes the most productive thing you can do.

Reflection Questions for Chapter 3

1. What is your honest relationship with exercise? What emotions come up when you think about moving your body?
2. What form of movement brought you joy in the past? Could you return to it now?
3. What is your biggest barrier to consistent exercise? Is it truly insurmountable, or is it an excuse you've accepted?
4. When during the day do you have the most natural energy? How could you leverage that time for movement?
5. Who could serve as your accountability partner? Who would you not want to disappoint by skipping a workout?

Chapter 3 Action Items

This Week:

- Walk for 10 minutes three times, just three ten-minute walks
- Identify one form of movement you actually enjoy
- Schedule exercise sessions in your calendar like any other important appointment
- Remove one barrier (pack gym bag, lay out clothes, identify location)

This Month:

- Build to five 30-minute cardiovascular sessions weekly
- Add two strength training sessions (bodyweight exercises count)
- Track how you feel after exercising, energy, mood, sleep quality

- Find one accountability partner or join one group fitness activity

This Quarter:

- Achieve consistency: five cardio sessions and two strength sessions weekly for at least eight consecutive weeks
- If you're approaching or past menopause, ensure you're lifting weights heavy enough to challenge your muscles
- Explore functional fitness exercises that support daily activities
- Notice changes in your body: increased stamina, better sleep, improved mood, easier daily tasks

Start Today:

Right now, before finishing this chapter, stand up. Walk around your house for five minutes. That's it. Five minutes of movement.

You've started.

Tomorrow, do it again.

The journey of building lifelong movement habits begins with five minutes today.

Part 3: Building Your External World

Chapter 4: Crafting Your Community: Intentional Relationships

"Iron sharpens iron." – Proverbs 27:17

You Are Shaped by Who You Spend Time With

There's a phenomenon in behavioral science that fascinates me: if your five closest friends are overweight, you're significantly more likely to be overweight yourself. If your friends are financially successful, you're more likely to achieve financial success. If your social circle values health and wellness, you'll naturally gravitate toward healthier choices.

This isn't about competition, though that can play a role. It's about influence, the subtle, constant shaping force of the people you surround yourself with.

I see this pattern constantly in my practice. When a patient commits to losing weight, I ask about their social circle. Do their friends exercise? Do they go out for drinks multiple times weekly? Do they cook healthy meals or default to fast food?

The answers predict outcomes more reliably than any diet plan I could prescribe.

Think about wealthy individuals. They don't just happen to accumulate money in isolation. They're embedded in networks of other successful people. They share accountants, investment strategies, business opportunities. They normalize wealth-building behaviors that seem foreign to those outside their circles.

The same principle applies to every dimension of life: health, relationships, career success, mental well-being. Your community either elevates you or anchors you in place.

This doesn't mean you should coldly evaluate friends based on their net worth or body mass index. It means you should be intentional about who influences your thoughts, choices, and daily habits.

When I was building my career, dealing with burnout, and redesigning my life, I became ruthless about my social circle. I needed drama-free friends. My peace was too precious to sacrifice for toxic relationships, no matter how long I'd known someone.

I cultivated friendships with people who celebrated wins rather than competing or feeling jealous. I sought out social, fun-loving friends who enjoyed dancing and laughter because that fed my soul. I maintained connections with intellectually stimulating friends, fellow physicians and book club members, who challenged my thinking.

I built multiple circles because different relationships serve different needs. My mother's group provides parenting support and shared experiences raising children. My physician colleagues understand the unique pressures of medicine. My book club friends offer intellectual stimulation and wine-fueled conversations that are frankly more entertaining than medical discussions.

We're social beings. We thrive in community. Isolation is becoming the new smoking, a public health crisis, especially among older adults. Loneliness kills as surely as cigarettes, increasing risk for heart disease, dementia, depression, and early death.

This is why intentionally crafting your community isn't optional. It's essential.

The Blue Zones: Community as Longevity

Remember the Blue Zones I mentioned in previous chapters, those regions where people routinely live past one hundred? Community is one of the five pillars of longevity in these populations.

In Okinawa, Japan, they have a concept called moai, social circles formed in childhood that provide lifelong support, companionship, and purpose. These groups meet regularly throughout life, celebrating together, grieving together, supporting each other through every season.

In Italy, family and community are woven into daily existence. Multiple generations live together or nearby. Older adults aren't isolated in nursing homes; they're integrated into family life, valued for their wisdom and experience.

Contrast this with American culture, where independence is celebrated above connection. We move away from family for careers. We place aging parents in assisted living facilities. We interact primarily through screens rather than face-to-face.

The result? An epidemic of loneliness and its devastating health consequences.

Some communities do this better. In certain cultures, bringing elderly family members into the home is expected and honored. These multi-generational households provide built-in social connection, purpose, and support.

I live about an hour and a half from my mother. Now that she's aging, that distance creates challenges. I can't be there constantly, so my brother and I collaborate. He handles day-to-day needs since he lives closer; I manage medical aspects since I'm a physician. We work together, but it's imperfect. I wish I lived closer. I wish our culture made family caregiving easier.

But within the constraints we face, we do our best. That's all any of us can do: make intentional choices about connection within the realities we inhabit.

Building Your Circles

I want you to think about your current friend groups. Not the people you follow on social media, but the humans you actually spend time with, whose voices you hear, whose presence shapes your days.

Do you have multiple circles serving different needs?

I have:

- ❑ Mother friends who understand the chaos and joy of raising children
- ❑ Physician colleagues who speak my professional language
- ❑ Exercise friends from group fitness classes who motivate me to show up
- ❑ Book club friends who stimulate my mind

- [ ] Childhood and college friends who knew me before I became "Dr. Nicole"

Each circle provides something distinct. If I only had one type of friend, I'd be missing essential nutrients for my soul.

Your circles don't need to look like mine. They need to reflect your needs and values.

Maybe you need creative friends who inspire your artistic side. Maybe you need adventure friends who push you to try new experiences. Maybe you need quiet, contemplative friends who discuss philosophy and spirituality.

Build diversity into your social architecture.

The Quality Question

Here's the assessment I use: after spending time with someone, do you feel better or worse?

Do you feel energized, inspired, supported, understood? Or do you feel drained, criticized, anxious, diminished?

I teach my daughters this principle constantly. Whether it's a friend, boyfriend, or anyone else, pay attention to how you feel in their presence and after you leave.

If someone consistently makes you feel worse about yourself, that person doesn't belong in your inner circle. I don't care how long you've known them or what history you share.

This applies to family too. Sometimes, even blood relatives need boundaries. If a family member is toxic, abusive, or chronically negative, you're allowed to limit contact. Obligation doesn't override your well-being.

Friends are there for a reason, a season, or a lifetime. I heard Mel Robbins articulate this beautifully: friendships are shaped by proximity, timing, and commonalities.

Proximity: A friend who lives in your city will naturally be more present in your daily life than someone across the country. When one of you moves, the friendship changes. That's normal.

Timing: If you bond with someone while raising young children, then your kids grow up and that shared experience disappears, the friendship may naturally fade. You were aligned for that season but not necessarily for life.

Commonalities: Shared interests, values, life stages. When these shift, friendships shift too.

Understanding this framework releases you from guilt when friendships naturally evolve or end. You can appreciate what that person brought to your life during their season without forcing the relationship to continue artificially.

Sometimes it's okay to say: "That was a great friendship. We had a good run. Now we're in different places." Release with gratitude rather than resentment.

Making Friends as an Adult

Many patients tell me they struggle to make new friends as adults. I understand. It's harder than in childhood or college when proximity and timing automatically created opportunities.

But it's not impossible. You just have to be intentional and put yourself in positions where friendship can develop:

- ❑ Join group fitness classes, not just for exercise, but for community
- ❑ Take classes in subjects that interest you, cooking, art, writing, language
- ❑ Attend meetups centered on hobbies or interests
- ❑ Volunteer for causes you care about
- ❑ Join book clubs, running clubs, or other organized groups
- ❑ Connect with parents of your children's friends

The common thread: repeated exposure in low-stakes settings where conversation happens naturally.

You won't become best friends with everyone, but you'll create opportunities for connection. Some will stick, most won't. That's fine. You're looking for a few quality friendships, not popularity.

Put yourself out there. It's worth it. You need community to thrive.

Choosing Your Partner: The Most Important Decision

Now let's talk about the most important relationship you'll cultivate: your life partner.

If you're single and dating, this decision will shape every dimension of your future: where you live, whether you have children, your financial trajectory, your stress levels, your health, your happiness.

If you're already partnered, understanding what makes relationships work helps you strengthen what you have or recognize when something needs addressing.

Here's what I tell patients contemplating partnership: be intentional. Know yourself well enough to articulate what you need and what you absolutely cannot tolerate.

Your Top Ten Non-Negotiables

Before you can choose the right partner, you must identify your non-negotiables, the qualities or values you cannot compromise on.

My list would include:

1. Shared values around health and wellness (exercises regularly, doesn't smoke or use drugs)
2. Financial responsibility and aligned money beliefs
3. Desire for children (or not) with agreement on parenting approaches
4. Emotional maturity and communication skills
5. Religious or spiritual alignment (or at least respect for differences)
6. Supportive rather than competitive or jealous
7. Treats me with consistent kindness and respect

8. Makes me feel better in their presence, not worse
9. Similar social preferences (introverted vs. extroverted)
10. Shared vision for lifestyle (where to live, career priorities, retirement dreams)

Your list will differ based on what matters most to you. The point is having clarity before you're emotionally invested.

Know your deal-breakers too: abuse of any kind, addiction, dishonesty, fundamental value misalignments.

When you know your non-negotiables, you won't waste years trying to force relationships with incompatible people. You'll recognize red flags early and have courage to walk away.

Dating with Intention

If you're navigating online dating, which most people are these days, your non-negotiables become your filter.

Don't swipe on someone just because they're attractive. Read their profile. Do their stated values align with yours? Do they want children if you do (or don't)? Do they prioritize health? Do they have stable employment and financial responsibility?

I know this sounds clinical. Romance should be spontaneous and magical, right?

Here's the truth: the most successful, enduring marriages combine emotional connection with practical compatibility. You need both chemistry and alignment on life fundamentals.

Passion fades. Everyone who's been married long enough knows this. What sustains partnership is shared values, mutual respect, effective communication, and commitment to working through difficulties together.

If you build your relationship on shared foundations, intimacy and passion can be rekindled when they inevitably wane. If you build only on attraction, you have nothing to sustain you when the initial intensity fades.

Healing Your Baggage

Before you can be a good partner, you need to address your own wounds. We all carry baggage from childhood, previous relationships, trauma, and disappointments.

If you don't process this pain, you'll project it onto your partner. You'll interpret their neutral actions through the lens of your past hurts. You'll create conflicts where none need exist.

I strongly advocate for therapy, especially before entering serious relationships. Understand your attachment style. Recognize your triggers. Learn healthy communication patterns. Develop emotional regulation skills.

You want to enter partnership as a whole person who adds value, not as a broken person seeking someone to fix you.

A partner can't heal your childhood wounds. A partner can't cure your insecurities. A partner can't give you purpose or self-worth.

You must cultivate those things independently. Then you bring your whole self to meet their whole self, two complete people choosing to build something together rather than two halves desperately seeking completion.

If You're Already Partnered

What if you're already married or in a committed relationship? How do you strengthen what you have?

Communication is everything. Most relationship failures stem from inability to communicate effectively about needs, feelings, conflicts, and desires.

If you don't have strong communication skills, learn them. Read books. Attend workshops. Get couples therapy, not as a last resort when divorce is imminent, but as preventive maintenance for your relationship.

My husband and I do date night every Friday when his schedule allows. We protect that time fiercely. We also exercise together, travel together, pray together, and intentionally create shared experiences.

These practices keep us connected despite demanding careers and the exhaustion of parenting. We're not perfect, no relationship is, but we're committed to nurturing what we've built.

If your relationship isn't perfect now, ask yourself: what's in my power to improve it? Often we focus on what our partner should change while ignoring our own contributions to dysfunction.

Change what you can control. Communicate about the rest. If needed, seek professional support. Don't let pride or shame prevent you from getting help.

Designing Your Family Life

As you build your partnership, you're simultaneously designing your family life. These decisions deserve intentional thought:

- ❑ Where do you want to live? City, suburbs, rural area? Near family or far away?
- ❑ Do you want children? How many?
- ❑ How will you handle careers and childcare?
- ❑ What values will you prioritize in raising children?
- ❑ How will you manage finances jointly?
- ❑ How will you divide household responsibilities?
- ❑ What does your ideal daily life look like?

I'm not suggesting you need every answer before committing. Life surprises us. Plans change. But having conversations about these questions reveals whether you're fundamentally aligned or heading toward inevitable conflict.

I've seen too many patients in unhappy marriages because they never discussed critical issues before marriage. She assumed they'd live near her family; he assumed they'd relocate for his career. She wanted three children; he wanted none. She's a spender; he's a saver.

These misalignments create resentment, conflict, and sometimes divorce.

Have the hard conversations early. It's easier to end a dating relationship over incompatibility than to divorce after years of marriage and children.

The Drama-Free Requirement

I said earlier that I require drama-free friendships. The same applies to romantic relationships.

Life provides enough genuine stress: work pressures, health problems, financial challenges, family crises. You don't need to add relationship drama on top of that.

Drama means: constant conflict, jealousy, game-playing, emotional volatility, inconsistency, lack of trust.

Healthy relationships are peaceful foundations that support you through life's inevitable storms. They don't generate additional chaos.

If your relationship is a constant source of stress, something's wrong. Either the relationship is unhealthy, or one or both of you need to develop better skills.

Don't tolerate chronic drama. Don't normalize dysfunction. Peaceful, stable partnerships are possible. Don't settle for less.

Social Connection and Physical Health

Let me return to my physician perspective for a moment. Social connection isn't just about emotional well-being; it directly impacts physical health.

Studies show that strong social connections:

- ❑ Lower blood pressure
- ❑ Strengthen immune function
- ❑ Reduce inflammation
- ❑ Decrease risk of depression and anxiety
- ❑ Improve recovery from illness

- ❑ Extend lifespan

Conversely, loneliness and social isolation:

- ❑ Increase risk of heart disease by 29%
- ❑ Increase risk of stroke by 32%
- ❑ Increase dementia risk by 50%
- ❑ Are as harmful to health as smoking 15 cigarettes daily

This isn't soft science. This is hard data showing that relationships are as critical to health as diet and exercise.

When I see elderly patients who are isolated, I worry. I refer them to senior centers, community programs, religious organizations, anything to create social connection.

When I see young patients glued to screens, interacting primarily through social media, I worry differently. They have hundreds of online "friends" but feel profoundly lonely because digital connection doesn't provide the same neurological and physiological benefits as face-to-face interaction.

We need physical presence. We need eye contact. We need touch. We need the full sensory experience of being with other humans.

The Technology Problem

I can't discuss community without addressing social media's impact on relationships.

Social media promised connection but often delivers isolation. We scroll through curated highlight reels of others' lives, comparing our messy reality to their filtered fiction. We experience FOMO (fear of missing out) while simultaneously withdrawing from actual social engagement.

I see this destroying mental health, especially in young people.

There was a tragic case of an influencer, a young woman whose social media portrayed constant happiness: traveling, dining at restaurants, radiating joy. She committed suicide. Behind the perfectly curated feed was severe depression. She was faking it, and the performance became unbearable.

Online friends are not the same as real friends. Virtual community cannot replace physical community.

Video games are replacing outdoor play for young boys. TikTok is replacing conversation for teenagers. People don't know how to be bored anymore. Boredom used to drive us toward others, toward creativity, toward real engagement.

Now we fill every empty moment with scrolling.

When I was young, there was no internet. When I got bored, I talked to my parents. I was close with both of them because we had time and space for conversation. My grandfather lived with us. Multi-generational connection was normal.

Today's children grow up isolated in their devices. Parents are on phones. Kids are on phones. Everyone's physically present but emotionally absent.

If you have children, limit screen time, yours and theirs. Create phone-free zones: dinner table, bedrooms, family time. Model the behavior you want to see.

For yourself, notice how much time you spend scrolling versus actually connecting with people. Could you text a friend to meet for coffee instead of liking their Instagram post? Could you call someone instead of commenting on their status?

Real connection requires effort. It requires putting down the phone and being present.

The Gender Dynamics of Friendship

Here's something interesting I've noticed: men and women form friendships differently.

I used to think men were simpler, less dramatic, more straightforward. In some ways, that's true. Male friendships often form around shared activities rather than emotional processing.

But I'm learning that men face their own friendship challenges. Modern masculinity is shifting. Men are becoming more emotionally expressive, which is healthy, but they're also navigating new social dynamics.

One of my friends insists that men gossip more than women. I haven't researched this scientifically, but anecdotally, I hear it from multiple generations. My younger colleagues confirm that male social dynamics are more complex than previous generations experienced.

The point isn't to debate which gender struggles more with friendship. The point is that everyone needs intentional strategies for building and maintaining meaningful relationships.

Men: if you don't have close friends you can be vulnerable with, seek them out. Emotional suppression damages health.

Women: if your friendships are primarily surface-level or performance-based, dig deeper. Authenticity creates real connection.

Writing Your Intention for Community

I believe in writing intentions, making your desires concrete rather than leaving them vague.

Take time to write out your intention for your ideal community:

- ❑ What qualities do you want in friends?
- ❑ What activities do you want to share with friends?
- ❑ How often do you want to connect?
- ❑ What values must be shared?
- ❑ What boundaries do you need?

For romantic partnership, write even more specifically:

- ❑ What qualities does your ideal partner possess?
- ❑ How do they treat you?
- ❑ How do they handle conflict?
- ❑ What do they value?
- ❑ What lifestyle do you build together?

This isn't manifestation woo-woo. It's clarity. When you know what you're looking for, you recognize it when you find it. You also recognize what doesn't align and have courage to walk away.

I wrote intentions for my friendships, my marriage, my family life. It helped me design rather than default.

You can do the same.

When Community Feels Hard

Maybe you're reading this thinking: "This sounds great, but I'm struggling. I'm lonely. I don't know how to connect. I've been hurt before and I'm scared to try again."

I understand. Building community requires vulnerability. It risks rejection. It takes time.

Start small. One connection. One conversation. One step toward others.

If you're dealing with significant social anxiety or trauma around relationships, work with a therapist. These are learned skills. If you didn't learn them growing up, you can learn them now.

Remember: everyone feels awkward initiating friendship. Everyone fears rejection. You're not alone in that fear.

Most people want connection as much as you do. They're waiting for someone to make the first move. That someone can be you.

Invite a coworker to coffee. Text an old friend you've lost touch with. Join one group. Show up consistently.

Connection builds slowly through repeated low-stakes interactions. Trust develops over time. You don't have to rush it.

The Community Assessment

Look at your current life honestly:

Are you isolated or connected?

Do you have people you can call at 3 AM if you need help?

Do you have people who know you deeply, who've seen you at your worst and love you anyway?

Do you have diverse friendships that feed different parts of you?

Are your relationships reciprocal, or are you always giving or always taking?

Do you feel energized or drained by your social life?

Your answers reveal where you need to focus.

If you're isolated, prioritize connection above almost everything else. Your health depends on it.

If you're surrounded by toxic relationships, start creating distance and building healthier connections simultaneously.

If you have great friendships, maintain them. Don't take them for granted. Friendships require ongoing investment.

The Practice of Showing Up

The most important principle for building community: show up consistently.

Show up when it's convenient and when it's not.

Show up when you feel like it and when you don't.

Show up for celebration and for grief.

Show up in person when possible, not just through text.

Relationships deepen through consistent presence.

If your friend is going through a hard time, don't just say "let me know if you need anything." They won't ask. Show up with food. Offer specific help: "I'm running errands on Tuesday, what can I get you?"

If your friend has good news, celebrate genuinely without making it about yourself or comparing.

Be the friend you want to have. That's how you attract quality people.

A Note on Toxic Positivity

I want to distinguish between healthy relationships and toxic positivity.

Healthy relationships allow space for struggle, sadness, anger, fear. You can be real. You don't have to perform happiness.

Toxic positivity demands that you always be fine, always look on the bright side, never burden anyone with genuine difficulty.

That's not community. That's performance.

Real community holds space for your full humanity. When you're struggling, real friends sit with you in that struggle. They don't try to fix it or minimize it or tell you to just think positive.

They witness your pain and stay present.

That's what you deserve. That's what you should offer others.

Your Community as Your Legacy

The relationships you build become part of your legacy. Not just romantic partnership and children, but the friendships you cultivate, the community you contribute to, the lives you touch.

When you're eighty-five, you won't remember how many Instagram followers you had. You'll remember the people who showed up, who laughed with you, who cried with you, who made life worth living.

Invest in those relationships now.

Make time even when you're busy. Especially when you're busy.

Prioritize presence over productivity sometimes.

Choose people over screens.

Choose depth over breadth.

Build your community with the same intentionality you bring to your career, your health, your finances.

Because here's the truth that took me years to learn: success means nothing if you're alone. Health means less if you have no one to share your life with. Money can't buy genuine connection.

The richest life, the one where you truly thrive, is built on relationships that sustain, challenge, celebrate, and see you.

That's the community worth crafting.

***

In the next chapter, we'll explore how to design your career and financial future, ensuring that your work aligns with your values and your money supports the life you're intentionally building.

Reflection Questions for Chapter 4

1. Who are the five people you spend the most time with? How do they influence your choices, health, mindset, and life direction?
2. After spending time with each person in your inner circle, do you generally feel better or worse? What does that tell you?
3. What qualities are non-negotiable for you in close friendships? In romantic partnership?
4. Are your current relationships reciprocal, or are you consistently giving more (or taking more) than you receive?
5. How much time do you spend on social media versus face-to-face interaction? Is that balance serving you?
6. What barriers prevent you from building the community you want? Are they real constraints or fears you could address?
7. If you're in a romantic relationship, are you actively nurturing it with communication, shared experiences, and intentional time together?
8. Write your intention: What does your ideal community look like? What qualities do you want in your closest relationships?

Chapter 4 Action Items

This Week:

- ❑ Evaluate your current friendships honestly: energizing or draining?
- ❑ Reach out to one person you've lost touch with
- ❑ Put your phone away during one social interaction and be fully present
- ❑ If you're partnered, schedule one date or quality time activity
- ❑ Limit social media to 30 minutes daily and notice how you feel

This Month:

- ❑ Join one group activity that interests you (fitness class, book club, volunteer opportunity)
- ❑ If you're single and dating, write your top 10 non-negotiables for partnership
- ❑ If you're partnered, have one important conversation you've been avoiding
- ❑ Invite someone to coffee or a walk, initiate connection
- ❑ Attend one community event (religious service, neighborhood gathering, local meetup)
- ❑ Call three friends just to check in, no agenda required

This Quarter:

- ❑ Build at least one new meaningful connection through consistent showing up

- [ ] If toxic relationships exist in your life, create boundaries or distance
- [ ] Develop or strengthen diverse friend circles that serve different needs
- [ ] If you're experiencing loneliness, see a therapist to address barriers to connection
- [ ] Plan one shared experience with your community: group trip, dinner party, volunteer day
- [ ] Write detailed intentions for your ideal friendships and romantic partnership

Start Today:

- [ ] Choose the smallest possible action. Text one person right now to tell them you appreciate them. Schedule one coffee date. Join one online community for your interests. Make one phone call instead of sending a text.
- [ ] Community doesn't build itself. It requires intention, vulnerability, consistency, and courage.
- [ ] You don't have to do this perfectly. You just have to start.
- [ ] Your people are out there. The community you crave is possible.
- [ ] It begins with one step toward connection.
- [ ] Take that step today.

Chapter 5: Designing Your Career and Financial Future

"Money doesn't buy happiness, but it helps."

, Unknown

The Conversation No One Had With Me

I remember standing outside a house in La Jolla when I was in junior high, peering through the windows at what seemed like another universe. My friend's father was the CEO of a major corporation, and their home had a pool, a sprawling garden, rooms that seemed to unfold endlessly. I wasn't jealous, that's not the right word. I was curious. I thought,

This is nice. I want this for myself. Why not?

That afternoon planted something in me that took decades to fully understand. It wasn't about the pool or the square footage. It was about choices. Those kids had options I didn't even know existed. Summer programs that cost a thousand dollars. Extracurricular activities that required fees my single mother couldn't conjure. Social groups that seemed reserved for families with resources I couldn't name.

I grew up in subsidized housing in San Diego. My mother was divorced, raising me on her own, stretching every dollar until it screamed. We weren't on food stamps, but we were close enough to that line that I learned early what it meant to not have access. I remember desperately wanting to attend a freshman summer program at UCLA, a thousand-dollar investment that would have given me a head start, connections, friendships that formed while I was still on the waitlist of belonging.

"Mom, please," I begged. "Is there any way?"

She looked at me with that expression parents wear when they're breaking their own hearts. "I don't have a thousand dollars. I just don't have it."

When I arrived at UCLA that fall, everyone else had already formed their tribes. They had inside jokes from summer orientation, study groups already established, a social foundation I spent the entire first semester trying to build from scratch. That memory became a promise I made to myself: I would never be in that position again. Not for myself. Not for my future children.

Here's what no one told me growing up: financial health is health. It reverberates through every dimension of your life, your stress levels, your sleep, your access to nutritious food, your neighborhood, your children's schools, even which doctors you can see and what treatments are available to you. As a physician, I witness this daily. Patients with government insurance don't have access to the same specialists, the same medications, the same preventive care as those with better coverage. Money doesn't just buy things. Money buys choices.

And yet, in all my years of schooling, thirteen years of higher education to become a physician, no one ever taught me about money.

Not in elementary school. Not in high school. Not in college or medical school. We learn calculus and chemistry, literature and Latin, but we graduate into adulthood financially illiterate, expected to navigate a system no one explained.

This chapter is the conversation I wish someone had with me.

Money as Medicine

In my practice, I see the health consequences of financial stress every single day. The patient who can't afford organic produce and subsists on processed food because it's cheaper. The mother who skips her own medications to pay for her children's. The worker who stays in a toxic job because he can't afford the gap between paychecks if he leaves. The woman who hasn't taken a vacation in four years and sits in my office with depression, anxiety, and memory problems that I'm certain are rooted in chronic, unrelenting stress.

Poverty isn't just an economic condition. It's a health condition. Research consistently shows that financial instability correlates with higher rates of heart disease, diabetes, depression, and early death. When you're living paycheck to paycheck, your cortisol levels remain chronically elevated. Your body stays in fight-or-flight mode. You don't sleep well. You make food choices based on cost rather than nutrition. You delay medical care until small problems become emergencies.

This is why I include financial wellness in a book about thriving. You cannot design your best life without addressing money. Not because money equals happiness, research is clear that beyond a certain threshold, additional wealth doesn't increase wellbeing. But because lacking financial stability creates a constant undercurrent of anxiety that undermines everything else you're trying to build.

Money is more choices. Let me say that again: money is more choices. The choice to leave a bad relationship because you're not financially dependent on your partner. The choice to take time off when you're burned out. The choice to send your children to better schools. The choice to eat whole foods. The choice to see specialists. The choice to travel, to rest, to pursue passions that don't pay. The choice to give generously to causes you believe in.

My father, a preacher, raised me with the verse that money is the root of all evil. He refused payment for his ministry, remaining poor as a matter of principle. I respect his conviction, but I've come to a different understanding. Money itself is neutral, it's a tool. Like food, like exercise, like anything else, it becomes problematic only when it's misused, hoarded, or pursued at the expense of everything that matters. But used wisely? Money is medicine. It's freedom. It's the ability to build a legacy that outlasts you.

The Architecture of Financial Health: The 50-30-20 Framework

I'm going to give you the simplest possible framework for managing money. It's not the only approach, and as you grow financially, you'll develop more sophisticated strategies. But if you do nothing else, if you remember nothing else from this chapter, remember this: 50-30-20.

Fifty percent of your income goes to needs. These are your essentials, housing, utilities, transportation, groceries, insurance, minimum debt payments. The non-negotiables that keep your life functioning.

Thirty percent goes to wants. This is the category that trips people up because the line between needs and wants is blurrier than we admit. Dining out isn't a need; cooking at home is. A basic phone plan is a need; the latest smartphone is a want. Your wants include entertainment, hobbies, travel, gym memberships, streaming subscriptions, that morning coffee you buy instead of brewing at home. These aren't bad expenditures, they're what makes life enjoyable. But they must fit within the thirty percent.

Twenty percent goes to savings and debt repayment. This is where you build your future. Retirement contributions, emergency fund, paying down credit card balances beyond the minimum, investments. This category is non-negotiable. It's paying yourself first.

Here's what I want you to understand: this framework isn't restrictive. It's liberating. When you know exactly what you have available for wants, you can spend that money without guilt. You can enjoy your dinner out, your vacation, your new clothes, because you've already allocated for your needs and your future. The anxiety around spending disappears when you have a system.

I use a simple paper budget sheet I got from an old accountant years ago. Every month, I write out my income and expenses. I know exactly where my money goes. Some people use apps; some use spreadsheets; some ask ChatGPT to create a budget based on their salary and expenses. The method doesn't matter. What matters is awareness. If you don't know where your money goes, it simply goes, usually toward things that don't bring lasting satisfaction.

Your Financial Safety Net: The Emergency Fund

Before you invest a single dollar, before you think about retirement accounts or stock portfolios, you need an emergency fund. Three to six months of living expenses, sitting in a regular savings account where you can access it immediately.

This money isn't for investing. It's for sleeping at night.

Life happens. Your car breaks down. Your roof leaks. You get laid off. You have a medical emergency. Many disability insurance policies have ninety-day waiting periods, that's where your three-month cushion becomes essential. Without an emergency fund, unexpected expenses go on credit cards, accumulating interest, creating a debt spiral that can take years to escape.

If you're currently living paycheck to paycheck, that's a sign your financial health needs attention. I say this without judgment, I understand the circumstances that lead there. But I also know it's possible to change. Start with one month of expenses as your first goal. Then two. Then three. Build slowly but consistently. That cushion represents more than money. It represents security. It represents breathing room. It represents the ability to make decisions from a place of stability rather than desperation.

Credit: The Game You Must Play Wisely

Your credit score is a report card that follows you through adult life. When you buy a car, it determines your interest rate. When you buy a home, it determines whether you qualify and at what cost. When you rent an apartment, landlords check it. When you apply for certain jobs, employers review it.

A score of 700 or above is considered good. You build credit by taking out loans and paying them on time, car payments, mortgage payments, credit cards. You damage credit by carrying high balances, missing payments, having too many accounts, or maxing out your available credit.

Credit cards are tools, not traps, but only if you have discipline. If you can pay your balance in full every month, credit cards offer convenience and often rewards. I use credit cards with travel perks for most purchases, accumulating points that fund vacations. But I pay off the balance every month. I never carry debt. The moment you start carrying a balance, the interest rates, often 20% or higher, begin eroding your financial health.

I remember my first week at UCLA. Credit card companies had tables everywhere during orientation, offering free t-shirts and pizza to sign up. Students with no income were suddenly handed cards with thousand-dollar limits. By semester's end, many had maxed them out, beginning their adult lives in debt.

If you're not disciplined enough to pay off your credit card every month, you don't need a credit card. Cut it up. Use cash or debit. Build that discipline before adding credit back into your life.

Automate everything possible. Bill payments, credit card payments, savings transfers. Automation removes the risk of forgetfulness and ensures you're always paying on time. Late payments damage your credit score and cost you money in fees. Set it and forget it.

Retirement: Your Future Self Is Counting on You

The rule of thumb is to save ten to fifteen percent of your gross income for retirement. If your employer offers a 401(k) with matching contributions, contribute at least enough to get the full match, that's free money you're leaving on the table otherwise.

Here's a simple calculation called the 25x Rule: estimate how much you'll spend annually in retirement and multiply by twenty-five. If you expect to spend sixty thousand dollars per year, you need 1.5 million dollars saved. This assumes a standard thirty-year retirement, retire at sixty-five, live until ninety-five, and a safe withdrawal rate of four percent annually.

These numbers can feel overwhelming, especially if you're starting late. But time is your greatest asset. Money invested early compounds dramatically. A dollar invested at twenty-five is worth far more at retirement than a dollar invested at forty-five. Start where you are, with what you have, even if it feels insignificant. Consistent small contributions over decades build wealth you can't imagine.

If you don't have access to an employer-sponsored plan, open an Individual Retirement Account (IRA) through a company like Vanguard or Fidelity. Choose a target-date fund based on your expected retirement year, say, 2050 or 2055. These funds automatically adjust their asset allocation as you age, becoming more conservative as retirement approaches. It's a set-it-and-forget-it approach for people who don't want to actively manage investments.

The key is to make retirement savings automatic. Have it deducted from your paycheck before you ever see it. If you don't see it, you don't miss it. This is paying yourself first in action.

Your Career: More Than a Paycheck

Money matters, but career fulfillment matters too. I've seen too many patients destroy their health for jobs that pay well but drain their souls. They work sixty-hour weeks, skip meals, sacrifice sleep, neglect exercise, miss their children's milestones, all for a salary that can't buy back the years they've lost.

I speak from experience. My first physician jobs were miserable. I moved between clinics, always blaming external circumstances, until I finally burned out completely. The pressure was crushing, rushing from patient to patient, fifteen minutes per person, writing orders and notes, ten times a day, three exam rooms full plus a video call waiting, everyone needs you now. I gave a TEDx talk on physician burnout because I lived it.

What my burnout taught me was that career design is as essential as life design. I had to ask myself hard questions: Was I working too many hours? Was the environment toxic? Was I being paid fairly for my expertise? Were there opportunities for growth? Did my work align with my sense of purpose?

I redesigned my career. I transitioned to a four-day work week. I created clinic cultures that felt peaceful, family-like, drama-free. I diversified my income streams, faculty at a medical school, urgent care shifts, my hospital panel, a private practice in weight loss and wellness. What once felt like overwhelming pressure from one employer became a portfolio of purpose. Each role fulfills different needs. Together, they create both financial stability and professional satisfaction.

The Career Checkup

I recommend conducting a career checkup annually, asking yourself honest questions:

- Am I being paid fairly for my role and experience?
- Am I fulfilled by my work, or am I just going through the motions?
- Is my work environment healthy, physically and emotionally?
- Are there opportunities for growth, or have I plateaued?
- Does my schedule allow for exercise, sleep, meals, and family?
- If I look at my manager's position, do I want what they have?

If you're in a job that's detrimental to your health, if you're skipping meals, sacrificing sleep, too exhausted to exercise, something has to change. Either the job needs boundaries, or you need a different job.

I know people who've been in the same position for twenty years, stuck and complaining, as if their circumstances are immutable facts rather than choices they've unconsciously made. Here's what I believe: everyone is capable of learning more. And when you learn more, you earn more. If you want to advance, identify the skills required and acquire them. Take courses. Get certifications. Read voraciously. The investment in yourself always pays returns.

The Time Budget

We budget money, but we rarely budget time, and time is actually the more precious resource. You have twenty-four hours in a day. If you spend eight working and eight sleeping, you still have eight hours remaining. What are you doing with them?

Are you exercising? Learning? Connecting with people you love? Pursuing hobbies that restore your soul? Or are you scrolling social media, watching television, falling down rabbit holes that leave you feeling emptier than before?

Your career can be purposeful and fulfilling, or it can simply be the means to fund the things you truly love. Either approach is valid. But know which you've chosen. If your job is a means to an end, make sure you're actually using your non-work hours to pursue that end. If your job is supposed to be fulfilling but isn't, recognize the misalignment and address it.

I believe we're born for a purpose, and that purpose involves sharing our talents with the world to make it better. Some people know their purpose early. For others, it reveals itself over time. But living by default, without intention, without goals, without direction, leads to bad habits, addiction, passivity. It leads to sitting on the couch eating mindlessly while the television drones, days blurring into weeks into years of unrealized potential.

Multiple Streams: Don't Put All Your Eggs in One Basket

For years, I had one source of income: my salary from a single employer. When that relationship became strained, when the pressure became unsustainable, I felt trapped. I needed that paycheck. I couldn't afford to leave.

Now I understand the value of diversification. Just as you shouldn't invest all your retirement savings in one stock, you shouldn't depend entirely on one income source. Multiple streams of income provide security and flexibility. If one source dries up, others sustain you. If one job becomes toxic, you have options.

Think about what additional income streams you could create. A side business based on a skill you have. Consulting work in your area of expertise. Rental income from property. Investment dividends. Freelance projects. Teaching or tutoring. The internet has made it easier than ever to monetize skills and passions.

I'm not suggesting you work yourself into exhaustion with multiple jobs. I'm suggesting you build resilience into your financial life. Even modest additional income, a few hundred dollars monthly from a side project, adds up over time and provides psychological security beyond its dollar amount.

The Art of Living Below Your Means

Social media has created a particularly toxic phenomenon: we compare our everyday lives to everyone else's highlight reels. We see friends' vacations, their new cars, their designer clothes, their restaurant meals. We don't see their credit card balances, their anxiety about bills, their financial stress hidden behind curated images.

Keeping up with the Joneses is a recipe for financial disaster. Living above your means, spending more than you earn, financing lifestyle on credit, leads to a debt spiral that can take decades to escape. The anxiety of owing money, of watching interest accumulate, of knowing you're falling further behind each month, this is a form of chronic stress that damages health as surely as any disease.

I love to shop. I love to travel. I enjoy nice things. But I've learned to pursue these pleasures strategically. I buy clothes at consignment stores, designer items at a fraction of retail. My children have learned this too; they find jeans that cost one hundred dollars retail for twenty dollars at resale shops. I drive a used car, not the latest model. I travel during off-seasons when prices drop dramatically. I choose destinations where my dollar stretches further, Portugal instead of Hawaii, where a dinner with wine costs forty euros instead of two hundred dollars.

People sometimes comment that I travel a lot, that I seem to do a lot of things. What they don't see is the strategy behind it. I travel three times for what others spend on one "dream vacation" because I'm not chasing luxury, I'm chasing experiences. I save on some things so I can spend on others.

Figure out what actually brings you joy and spend there. Cut ruthlessly in areas that don't matter to you. This is financial intentionality, the same principle we apply to time, relationships, and health.

Teaching the Next Generation

I started working at fourteen, babysitting, newspaper routes, whatever jobs would have me. I worked because I wanted things my mother couldn't provide: a car, clothes, experiences. Working taught me that money comes from effort, that desires require action, that the world is transactional.

Now, as a parent, I'm intentional about teaching my children these lessons. They have chores, and they receive allowance for completing them, the connection between work and compensation established early. I provide their basic needs, but wants come from their own earnings. When they want something extra, they understand they need to save for it.

My oldest is now a college freshman. I've been transparent with her about the family finances, here's what we're contributing to your education, here's what it costs, here's the value of what you're receiving. I've encouraged her to get a part-time job, not for the money alone, but to start building credit, to understand the relationship between time and income, to begin the long education in financial adulthood that school won't teach her.

I share my credit score with my children. I show them how credit cards work, how I use them for rewards but pay them off monthly. I want them to arrive at adulthood financially literate, armed with knowledge I had to acquire through books and mistakes.

Goals, Vision, and the Power of Writing It Down

Every year, I create a vision board. I write down goals for my health, my wealth, my relationships, my personal growth. My family does this together, a ritual of intention-setting that shapes our year.

People dismiss vision boards as woo-woo nonsense, but here's what I've observed: the act of articulating what you want forces clarity. When you write a goal, you've committed to it in a way that vague wishing never achieves. You've made it concrete. You can measure progress against it.

Even if you accomplish only fifty percent of what you envision, that's fifty percent more than if you'd never set goals at all. You move from zero to somewhere. That somewhere compounds over years into a life you've actually designed rather than defaulted into.

I think of Steve Jobs starting Apple in his garage. Jeff Bezos launching Amazon from a similar humble origin. These aren't just inspirational stories, they're examples of what happens when vision meets persistence. Apple didn't succeed immediately; there were years of struggle. But Jobs had a goal, a vision, and he worked toward it relentlessly.

You don't need to build the next Apple. But you do need goals. One-year goals. Five-year goals. Ten-year goals. Where do you want to be financially? What income would give you the life you want? What would need to change to get there?

Write it down. Put it somewhere you'll see it. Let it guide your decisions.

Generosity: The Highest Use of Wealth

In November 2024, Mackenzie Scott donated sixty-three million dollars to Howard University, where I went to medical school, including seventeen million specifically to the College of Medicine. I saw that announcement and wept.

Howard is where I became a doctor. I wasn't the strongest candidate when I applied, coming from humble beginnings meant I didn't have the best test scores, the most impressive extracurriculars, the polished preparation of wealthier applicants. HBCUs, historically Black colleges and universities, understand this. They see potential in students the system might overlook. They gave me a chance.

I received two alumni scholarships during medical school, gifts from graduates before me who wanted to help students like I was. I graduated with less debt because strangers believed in investing in the next generation. That's legacy. That's philanthropy in action.

Next year marks my twenty-five-year reunion from Howard, and I'm heading the committee to raise scholarship funds for incoming medical students. It brings my story full circle, from recipient of generosity to giver. I can't donate sixty-three million dollars. But I can contribute what I'm able. I can fundraise. I can help one student avoid the debt that might have crushed them.

Mackenzie Scott has donated over nineteen billion dollars to causes she believes in: HBCUs, Habitat for Humanity, Planned Parenthood, Girl Scouts. She has the wealth to make choices on a scale most of us can't imagine. But the principle applies regardless of your income level.

If you can be generous with your money, you should be. Not because you're obligated, but because generosity transforms both giver and receiver. It connects you to community. It provides purpose beyond personal consumption. It creates ripples you may never see but that extend further than you know.

If you don't have money to give, give time. Volunteer. Mentor. Share knowledge. The world needs what you have to offer, whether that's dollars or hours or expertise.

But remember: you must secure your own oxygen mask first. You can't give from an empty well. Build your financial stability, then build your generosity on that foundation.

Work Hard, Play Hard

That's my motto, and I make no apologies for it.

I work hard because I remember what it felt like to not have options. I remember the summer program I couldn't attend. The social groups I couldn't join. The choices that weren't available to me because my mother didn't have a thousand dollars.

I play hard because life is for living, not just earning. The travel I do, the experiences I create for my family, the joy I find in a Portuguese dinner that costs forty euros, these are the returns on my investment. This is what the hard work purchases.

Dreams come true when they're paired with goals and action. Everyone who achieved something remarkable started somewhere ordinary. They had a vision. They worked toward it. They didn't wait until they were ready, until conditions were perfect, until someone gave them permission.

We live in America, for all its flaws, a place where hard work can still change your circumstances. I grew up in subsidized housing. I am now a physician, a medical school faculty member, a business owner, an author. Not because I'm exceptional, because I was intentional. Because I set goals and pursued them relentlessly. Because I learned what no one taught me and applied it consistently.

You can do the same.

The recipes in this chapter are simple. Following them isn't always easy, I won't pretend otherwise. But the principles are clear: live below your means, save consistently, build an emergency fund, manage credit wisely, invest in your future self, diversify income, spend intentionally, give generously, and never stop learning.

Financial health is health. It deserves the same attention you give to nutrition, to movement, to mental wellness. When all these dimensions align, body, mind, relationships, career, finances, that's when thriving becomes possible.

That's when you stop merely surviving and start designing a life that feels intentional, purposeful, and deeply your own.

Reflection Questions for Chapter 5

1. What is your earliest memory related to money? How might that experience have shaped your current financial beliefs and behaviors?
2. If you applied the 50-30-20 framework to your current income, where do your expenses actually fall? What adjustments would bring you into alignment?
3. Do you have an emergency fund? If not, what amount would you need to cover three months of essential expenses? What's one step you could take this week to start building it?
4. Conduct an honest career checkup: Are you fulfilled? Are you compensated fairly? Is your work environment healthy? What would need to change for you to answer "yes" to all three?
5. What brings you genuine joy when you spend money? What expenses do you make out of habit or social pressure rather than true enjoyment?
6. Where could you create an additional income stream using skills or passions you already have?
7. What's one area where you could live more below your means, not as deprivation, but as strategic redirection toward what matters more?
8. If you had complete financial security, how would your daily life change? What would you spend your time doing?

Chapter 5 Action Items

This Week

- ❑ Calculate your current spending against the 50-30-20 framework
- ❑ Check your credit score (free through many banks or services like Credit Karma)
- ❑ Automate one bill payment you've been paying manually
- ❑ Identify one "want" expense you could reduce or eliminate without genuine loss of enjoyment

This Month

- ❑ Create a written budget tracking all income and expenses
- ❑ Open a dedicated savings account for your emergency fund if you don't have one
- ❑ Set up automatic transfers to savings on each payday (start with whatever you can, even $25)
- ❑ If employed, verify you're maximizing any employer retirement match
- ❑ Conduct a career checkup using the questions in this chapter

This Quarter

- ❑ Build your emergency fund to at least one month of expenses
- ❑ Research one potential additional income stream and take the first step toward creating it

- [ ] Read one book about personal finance (recommendations: "I Will Teach You to Be Rich" by Ramit Sethi, "The Simple Path to Wealth" by JL Collins)
- [ ] Create a vision board or written goals document for your financial life
- [ ] Identify one cause you care about and make a contribution, of money or time

Start Today

Open your banking app or log into your accounts online. Look at your spending from the past month. Don't judge it, just observe. Awareness is the first step toward intentionality.

Then ask yourself one question: *Is this spending aligned with the life I'm trying to design?*

If yes, wonderful. Keep going.

If no, you now know where to focus.

Financial health, like physical health, isn't achieved through dramatic overnight transformation. It's built through small, consistent choices that compound over time.

Start where you are. Use what you have. Do what you can.

* * *

In the next chapter, we'll explore the final dimension of your designed life: embracing your authentic self. Because all the wealth, health, and success in the world means little if you haven't discovered who you truly are and what you're here to contribute.

Chapter 6: Embracing Your Authentic Self

"To know thyself is the beginning of wisdom."
, Socrates

The Question That Defined Me

I spent the first twenty years of my life not knowing where I came from.

I was born in the 1970s in San Diego, a love child of two military personnel, a white woman and a Black man, during an era when biracial children were still a rarity, when such unions drew stares and whispers. My birth mother was twenty-one, alone in her decision, and in a world less forgiving than today's, she did what she believed was best: she gave me up for adoption.

I was adopted as an infant by two Black parents. My adoptive mother was in her thirties, older, more established, eager for a daughter after her biological son. For a while, we were a family. Then, when I was still young, my parents divorced. My older brother, eleven years my senior, was their biological child. I was the adopted one. And suddenly I was being raised by a single mother in circumstances that required every dollar to stretch until it screamed.

Children who are adopted carry something specific in their psychology: a profound sense of abandonment. It doesn't matter how loving the adoptive home is, how devoted the parents who chose you. Somewhere in the architecture of your soul lives the knowledge that your first family gave you away. This shapes you in ways you don't fully understand until you're old enough to examine your own patterns, the relationships you choose, the fears that govern you, the relentless drive to prove yourself worthy of keeping.

I wasn't a social child. The world felt precarious, relationships felt temporary, and trust came slowly if it came at all. I learned early that if I wanted something, I would have to create it myself. No one was coming to rescue me. At fourteen, I started babysitting. Then came a newspaper route. By sixteen, I was working at the movie theater. By seventeen, I had graduated high school early and left for UCLA.

I loved being on my own. Making my own decisions, even when those decisions were mistakes. The mistakes were mine. The consequences were mine. The freedom was intoxicating.

But beneath all that fierce independence lived a question I couldn't answer: *Who am I?*

The Search for Origins

In my twenties, I hired a private investigator to find my birth mother.

The questions that had haunted me since childhood demanded answers. What did I look like as a baby? Where did my features come from? Was I a product of love, or violence? What was the story of my creation?

The investigator found her. She was living her life, still spiritual, still young at heart despite the decades that had passed. When we met, I understood things about myself I had never been able to name. We had the same face shape. The same hands. She had two sons, brothers I never knew existed. She was intelligent, curious, drawn to matters of faith and meaning.

I learned that I was, indeed, a love child. Not the product of violence or coercion, but of two young people who couldn't keep their hands off each other, something I witnessed firsthand when I brought my birth mother to meet my biological father for the first time in decades. They were drawn to each other magnetically, as if no time had passed, as if I weren't standing there observing this strange reunion of the people who had made me but never raised me.

My father was less interested in me than in reconnecting with my mother. I felt that sting, another echo of the original abandonment. But even that knowledge served a purpose: it explained something about my pattern of choosing unavailable men in my early relationships, my fear of being left, my tendency to love people who couldn't quite love me back.

Finding my birth parents didn't answer every question. But it filled in pieces of the puzzle that had been missing my entire life. I could see where my spirituality came from, my birth mother and I share that inclination toward the transcendent. I could understand my intellectual curiosity, my determination, the particular cast of my features that had never quite matched my adoptive family.

The woman who raised me, my adoptive mother, is my mother. That has never been in question. But meeting the woman who birthed me helped me understand the full story of who I am. Both truths exist simultaneously. Both shaped me.

The Layers of Identity

To be authentic is to know yourself. This sounds simple. It is not.

Identity is layered, complicated, shaped by forces we didn't choose. I am biracial in a country that has always been obsessed with race. I am a woman in a profession historically dominated by men. I am adopted in a culture that privileges biological connection. I am the daughter of a single mother in a society that still carries judgments about divorced families.

As African Americans, we face an additional complexity: the disconnection created by the slave trade severed our ancestral lines. I cannot trace my lineage back to a village in Ghana or Nigeria the way my white friends trace theirs to Ireland or Germany. The history was deliberately erased. Add adoption to that erasure, and the layers of not-knowing compound.

In my twenties, I went through a period of spiritual seeking. I explored Christianity, the faith I was raised in, my adoptive father being a preacher. I studied Kabbalah, Islam, Buddhism. I read voraciously, attended services and study groups, tried to understand what I believed and why. This wasn't a rejection of my upbringing; it was an attempt to choose my beliefs consciously rather than simply inheriting them by default.

That seeking was part of becoming authentic. When you examine your beliefs rather than accepting them passively, when you question rather than comply, you discover what actually resonates with your soul versus what you adopted to please others or fit in.

Now, in my forties, authenticity has become everything. I am attracted to people who are genuinely themselves, no masks, no performance, no pretense. I can sense inauthenticity almost immediately, perhaps because I spent so many years constructing versions of myself to navigate a world that felt unsafe.

The Practice of Knowing Yourself

How do you actually get to know yourself? This isn't a rhetorical question. It requires practice.

Start by observing. Pay attention to what energizes you and what depletes you. Notice when you feel most alive, most engaged, most yourself. Notice when you feel like you're performing, going through motions, wearing a mask you didn't consciously choose.

I am outgoing. I love to talk, to connect with people, to hear their stories and share my own. I am endlessly curious about human beings, what makes them tick, what they've survived, what they dream about. This aspect of my personality serves me well as a physician. Every patient is a story, and I want to understand all of it.

But I also know that too much social engagement exhausts me. I need solitude to recharge. I need quiet mornings and spa days and time when no one needs anything from me. Knowing this about myself means I can structure my life to honor both needs, the extroversion and the restoration.

I am highly motivated, productivity-oriented, prone to going and doing until I collapse. This trait built my career. It also created my burnout. Understanding that tendency means I can now set boundaries around it rather than letting it destroy me.

Think about how you know your children, if you have them. You know that this one likes to be put to bed a certain way, that one needs extra time to transition between activities, another one processes emotions by talking while another needs space. You've studied them. You understand their particular rhythms and needs.

We must study ourselves with the same attention. What are your rhythms? Your needs? Your breaking points? Your sources of restoration?

Self-Care as Self-Love

Knowing yourself creates the foundation for caring for yourself. And self-care is not indulgence, it's self-love in action.

When you truly understand your needs, you can meet them. When you know you need seven hours of sleep to function, you prioritize sleep rather than sacrificing it for one more episode or one more hour of scrolling. When you know that skipping exercise makes you irritable and foggy, you protect your workout time even when the calendar is screaming. When you know that certain foods make you feel terrible, you choose differently, not because someone told you to, but because you've learned what your body actually requires.

Self-care requires boundaries. This was one of my hardest lessons.

I am a physician. We are trained to sacrifice ourselves for patients, to work through exhaustion, to put our own needs last. There's nobility in service, but there's also destruction in martyrdom. I learned this the hard way.

My motto used to be "work hard, play hard." In practice, this meant grinding myself into the ground during the week, then collapsing into exhaustion on weekends. I would arrive at Palm Springs retreats barely able to walk, so depleted that I needed the first day just to recover from my own lifestyle. That's not thriving. That's survival punctuated by collapse.

I see this pattern constantly in my patients. They work seventy-hour weeks. They haven't taken a vacation in years. They skip meals, skip sleep, skip exercise. Then they arrive in my office wondering why they're depressed, why their memory is failing, why they have chronic headaches or digestive problems or fatigue that no amount of coffee can touch.

The answer is almost always the same: they've abandoned themselves. They've prioritized everything and everyone else until there's nothing left for their own wellbeing.

A forty-hour work week is already a lot. Beyond that, you're borrowing against your health, your relationships, your longevity. The interest rate on that loan is brutal.

Finding Environments That Honor Your Authentic Self

Authenticity isn't just internal. It requires environments that allow you to be yourself.

When I worked in corporate medicine, I felt like I couldn't be myself. The culture wanted cogs in a machine, interchangeable parts that processed patients efficiently, hit productivity targets, generated revenue. They didn't care that Nicole was passionate about her patients, that she wanted to spend extra time with someone who needed it, that she had insights beyond what could be captured in a fifteen-minute visit.

I was miserable. The money was good, but it didn't matter. My authentic self was being suffocated.

The problem was, I didn't know I had a choice. I had defaulted into that position because it was available, because the salary was attractive, because I thought this was simply what physicians did. I didn't realize I could design my career around my values rather than contorting myself to fit whatever opportunity appeared.

When I finally understood that I could choose, that I could deliberately create a four-day work week, build a clinic culture that felt peaceful and family-like, work in settings that aligned with who I am, everything changed.

This applies beyond careers. The relationships you're in, the city you live in, the social circles you inhabit, all of these either support your authentic self or suppress it. If you're constantly performing, constantly editing yourself, constantly feeling like you can't quite be who you are, that environment is wrong for you. Not wrong objectively. Wrong *for you*.

The Company You Keep

I love being around smart people. Not smart in a narrow, credential-based way, smart in the sense of curious, engaged, thinking about the world.

There's a study I read about that confirmed something I'd observed my entire life: when you surround yourself with intelligent, accomplished people, you unconsciously rise to meet them. Your standards elevate. Your thinking sharpens. You absorb perspectives and approaches you wouldn't have encountered in isolation.

This works in reverse too. If everyone around you is complacent, unmotivated, stuck in patterns of complaint without action, that energy pulls you down. You become what you surround yourself with.

I deliberately cultivate diverse friendships. I have physician friends who understand the specific challenges of medicine, the liability, the regulations, the emotional weight of holding people's lives in your hands. But I don't want to talk about medicine all the time. I need friends who think differently than I do.

I have a friend who's an attorney. Her mind works completely differently than mine. Conversations with her illuminate angles I would never have considered. I once had a colleague from a different political party than mine, genuinely, fundamentally different political beliefs. Our conversations were fascinating. I would think, "I never considered it that way. Now I understand why someone would hold that position."

Surrounding yourself with people who think exactly like you do is comfortable, but it's not growth. Your authentic self is developed through friction, through exposure to different perspectives, through having your assumptions challenged.

The Permission to Change Course

Here's something I wish someone had told me earlier: you're allowed to make mistakes. You're allowed to take U-turns.

When I was at UCLA, I dated an athlete. All the girls wanted athletes. It seemed like the thing to do. But I quickly realized that faithfulness wasn't part of that package. The culture around these men was one of options, of girls willing to accept what I wasn't willing to accept.

I knew myself well enough to recognize: this isn't going to work for me. I need someone who won't cheat. This environment, these norms, this pattern, it doesn't align with what I need.

So I pivoted. I stopped dating athletes. I changed direction.

That pivot changed my life. Not because dating athletes is inherently wrong, it worked fine for plenty of women, but because it was wrong for me. Knowing myself meant recognizing the misalignment early enough to correct course.

Think about driving. When you realize you're going the wrong direction, you don't just keep driving out of commitment to your original route. You turn around. You find your way back to where you need to go. Why would life be any different?

I've seen too many people stay in jobs, relationships, cities, entire life structures because they made a decision once and feel obligated to see it through. They chose this major, so they must work in this field. They married this person, so they must stay regardless of how destructive it's become. They bought this house, so they must live here even though they're miserable.

The sunk cost fallacy destroys authentic living. Your past decisions don't obligate your future self. You're allowed to evolve. You're allowed to learn. You're allowed to say, "That made sense then. It doesn't make sense now."

Breaking the Cycle of Default

The greatest enemy of authenticity is default. Living by default means accepting whatever circumstances present themselves rather than actively designing your life.

I lived by default for years. I took the job that was available. I dated whoever showed interest. I went wherever momentum carried me. Then I wondered why I was miserable, burned out, surrounded by situations that didn't fit who I actually was.

Default feels safe. It requires less effort than intentional choice. You don't have to risk rejection, failure, or the discomfort of change. You just... continue. One day blurs into the next, and suddenly you're forty-five years old living a life you never consciously chose.

I have a client who came from the projects. Her mother was a prostitute, absent more than present. Every external factor predicted that this woman would follow the same path. Instead, at seventeen, she left. She moved to a different city with no support, no resources, nothing but determination. She worked, saved, put herself through law school. Now she's a successful attorney.

Her circumstances didn't define her. She refused to let default dictate her destiny.

Not everyone can replicate her story. Structural barriers are real. Poverty is real. Systemic obstacles are real. But within whatever constraints you face, there is usually more room for choice than you believe. The first step is recognizing that choice exists, that you are not simply a product of your environment, but an agent capable of shaping your path.

The Voice That Knows

There is a voice inside you that knows what you need. Call it intuition, inner wisdom, your gut, the language doesn't matter. What matters is whether you listen.

This voice whispers at first. It's easy to ignore when you're busy, distracted, living at a pace that leaves no room for reflection. The job isn't right. The relationship isn't working. Something is off. You sense it but don't stop to examine it.

If you don't listen to the whisper, it gets louder. The dissatisfaction grows. The symptoms multiply. Eventually, what started as quiet discomfort becomes a crisis, burnout, breakdown, illness, the kind of dramatic rupture that forces change because you refused to make it voluntarily.

I've lived this pattern. I ignored the whispers about my corporate medicine job until my body gave me no choice. I ignored the whispers about relationships until the pain became undeniable. I learned the hard way that ignoring your inner voice doesn't make it go away. It just delays the reckoning and makes it more painful when it finally arrives.

Now I listen. When something feels wrong, I pay attention. I don't always act immediately, sometimes wisdom requires patience, but I no longer dismiss my own knowing.

Creating Your List of Joy

Part of knowing yourself is knowing what brings you joy. Not what should bring you joy, not what Instagram suggests should make you happy, but what actually lights you up.

My list: spa days, exercise, being outdoors, travel, reading, shopping at consignment stores for treasures other people have discarded, time with friends and family. When I structure my week to include these elements, I thrive. When I neglect them, I deteriorate.

What's on your list? Not what you think should be there. What actually is there, based on evidence from your own life?

When do you lose track of time? When do you feel most alive? When do you think, "I could do this forever"? Those moments reveal your authentic sources of joy.

I try to balance my week intentionally. Mondays and Tuesdays, when my energy is highest, I work intensively. As the week progresses, I wind down. I protect my days off fiercely. This isn't laziness, it's strategy. I've learned that my productivity and creativity depend on restoration. Grinding without pause produces diminishing returns.

The Commitment to Continuous Growth

Knowing yourself isn't a destination. It's an ongoing practice.

I am endlessly curious. I love learning. Just because I finished medical school and residency doesn't mean my education is complete. There is always something new in medicine, new research, new treatments, new understanding. There are always new fields to explore. When Bitcoin emerged, I read about it. When new investment strategies appeared, I studied them. When something interests me, I pursue it.

This curiosity is part of my authentic self. Honoring it means continuing to grow, refusing to calcify into the person I was ten years ago just because change requires effort.

The person you are at twenty-five is not the person you'll be at forty-five. Your authentic self evolves. New experiences shape you. Challenges transform you. Losses deepen you. The goal isn't to discover a fixed identity and defend it forever, it's to remain engaged in the ongoing process of becoming.

The Gift Your Authentic Self Offers the World

Think about what the world would lose if certain people hadn't lived their authentic lives.

What if Michael Jackson had suppressed his genius to fit into some conventional career path? What if he had listened to people who told him he was too different, too strange, too much? The joy his music brought to billions of people would never have existed.

What if Oprah had remained small, had accepted the limitations others tried to impose on a Black woman from Mississippi? The influence she's had, the lives she's touched, the conversations she's sparked, none of it would have happened.

Your authentic self has something to offer that no one else can provide. Not because you're uniquely talented or destined for fame, most of us aren't, but because your particular combination of experiences, perspectives, gifts, and wounds creates a contribution only you can make.

When you suppress your authentic self, you deprive the world of that contribution. When you live as a diminished version of yourself, performing, conforming, hiding, you withhold what you were meant to give.

This doesn't mean everyone should quit their job to pursue art or abandon all responsibilities in the name of self-expression. It means that within whatever life you're living, your authentic self deserves space. Your voice deserves to be heard. Your gifts deserve to be used.

The Journey Continues

I am still discovering who I am. At this point in my life, with my children growing, my career established, my understanding of myself far deeper than it was two decades ago, I am still learning. Still growing. Still becoming.

The adopted girl who didn't know where she came from has found her origins. The young woman who made mistakes in relationships has built a marriage. The physician who burned out has redesigned her career. The person who lived by default has learned to live by design.

But the journey isn't over. It never is.

My hope for you is that you engage in this journey with intention. That you ask the hard questions: Who am I? What do I need? What brings me joy? What drains me? What environments allow me to thrive? What relationships support my authentic self?

These questions don't have permanent answers. You'll answer them differently at different stages of life. But the practice of asking, of staying curious about yourself, of remaining willing to change course when something isn't working, is what allows you to live authentically rather than by default.

Your authentic self is not something you discover once and possess forever. It's something you cultivate, honor, protect, and express, daily, imperfectly, courageously.

It's the ongoing work of a lifetime.

It's the most important work there is.

* * *

In the next chapter, we'll explore the barriers that stand between you and the life you're designing, and how to break through them.

Reflection Questions for Chapter 6

1. What aspects of your identity were you born into versus chose consciously? How have inherited identities shaped your sense of self?
2. Are there questions about your origins or history that remain unanswered? How might seeking answers, or making peace with not knowing, affect your sense of authenticity?
3. What environments in your life (work, relationships, communities) allow you to be fully yourself? Which ones require you to perform or hide aspects of who you are?
4. When you listen to your inner voice, that whisper that knows what you need, what is it telling you right now? What have you been ignoring?
5. Where in your life are you living by default rather than by design? What would intentional choice look like in that area?
6. What brings you genuine joy, not what should bring you joy, but what actually does? When do you lose track of time?
7. Who are the people around you, and how do they influence your thinking, your standards, your sense of what's possible? Do these influences support or suppress your authentic self?
8. What U-turn might you need to take? What path that made sense once no longer serves who you're becoming?

Chapter 6 Action Items

This Week

- ❑ Write your "List of Joy", the activities, experiences, and conditions that genuinely bring you alive. Be honest, not aspirational.
- ❑ Identify one environment (job, relationship, social circle) where you feel you can't be fully yourself. What specifically feels inauthentic?
- ❑ Schedule one activity from your List of Joy this week, and protect that time.
- ❑ Notice one moment when you're performing rather than being genuine. Don't judge it, just observe.

This Month

- ❑ Audit your weekly schedule: How much time goes to obligations versus activities that align with your authentic self?
- ❑ Have one honest conversation with someone about something you've been hiding or minimizing.
- ❑ Identify one belief you hold because you inherited it versus chose it. Examine whether it still serves you.
- ❑ Seek out one person whose perspective differs significantly from yours. Have a genuine conversation.
- ❑ Set one boundary that honors your authentic needs, even if it disappoints someone.

This Quarter

- [ ] Make one significant change in an environment that suppresses your authentic self.
- [ ] Cultivate one new friendship with someone who challenges your thinking.
- [ ] If there are unanswered questions about your history or origins, take one step toward seeking answers.
- [ ] Evaluate your self-care practices: Are they actually caring for yourself, or are they performative?
- [ ] Identify one area where you're living by default and create a plan for intentional design.

Start Today

- [ ] Right now, ask yourself: *Am I being authentic in this moment?*
- [ ] Not yesterday. Not in general. Right now.
- [ ] If yes, notice what that feels like in your body. Remember it.
- [ ] If no, ask what would need to change for you to be more yourself in this moment.
- [ ] Authenticity isn't achieved through grand gestures. It's practiced in small moments, thousands of them, across the ordinary days of your life.
- [ ] This moment is one of them.
- [ ] What will you choose?

Chapter 7: Barriers and Breakthroughs

"The obstacle is the way."
, Marcus Aurelius

The Wall You Can't See

We've traveled far together in this book. You've learned about presence and intention, about nourishing your body with real food, about moving as medicine, about crafting community and designing your career. You've begun the deep work of embracing your authentic self.

And yet.

Something stops you. Maybe you've felt it while reading, a quiet resistance, a voice that whispers, "This sounds nice, but it won't work for me." Perhaps you've started making changes only to watch them dissolve within weeks. Maybe you're still standing at the starting line, book in hand, paralyzed by something you can't quite name.

That something is a barrier. And until you understand your barriers, truly understand them, breakthroughs remain frustratingly out of reach.

In my practice, I see this every day. Patients arrive with clear goals: lose weight, manage stress, sleep better, feel alive again. They leave with action plans, recommendations, prescriptions. Six months later, many return unchanged. Not because they didn't want transformation. Not because they lacked willpower. But because invisible barriers blocked their path, and no one had helped them see them.

This chapter is about seeing.

The Anatomy of Resistance

Barriers come in many forms, but they share a common feature: they feel like external obstacles when they're actually internal constructs. Understanding this distinction changes everything.

Fear is perhaps the most universal barrier. It masquerades as practicality: "I can't change jobs, the economy is uncertain." It disguises itself as responsibility: "I can't prioritize exercise, my family needs me." It hides behind logic: "Starting a business is too risky at my age."

But strip away the rationalizations, and fear is what remains. Fear of failure. Fear of success. Fear of judgment. Fear of the unknown.

I know this fear intimately because I've lived it.

My husband once observed something that stopped me cold. He said, "You operate from a childhood wound. You're always running, always earning, always securing, as if you're still that girl in subsidized housing, afraid of not having enough."

He was right. Growing up with a single mother, watching dollars stretch impossibly thin, missing opportunities because we couldn't afford them, these experiences etched patterns into my nervous system. Even now, decades later, with a successful career and financial stability, that fear whispers. It tells me to work more, save more, do more. It tells me that rest is dangerous, that slowing down invites disaster.

I estimate that fifty percent of the population carries some version of this wound. Financial insecurity in childhood creates a specific kind of fear that follows you into prosperity, that makes you work like you're still desperate even when desperation no longer applies.

The fear doesn't always announce itself. Sometimes it drives you unconsciously, and you don't realize you're running from something until someone holds up a mirror.

The Doing Disease

Last month, I returned from Portugal with a revelation that's still reshaping how I think about life.

In Lisbon, I sat at outdoor cafés watching people simply be. They weren't scrolling phones between bites. They weren't rushing to their next appointment. They were present, savoring wine, engaged in conversation, watching the world move at its natural pace. Meals lasted hours. Afternoons unfolded without urgency. People seemed to understand something Americans have forgotten: that productivity isn't the measure of a life well-lived.

I came home and looked at my own schedule, packed from morning to night, every hour accounted for, no buffer, no breathing room. My husband had been telling me for years: "You're always on a Zoom. You're always doing something." I had dismissed it as his laid-back temperament clashing with my driven nature.

But Portugal showed me the truth. Americans suffer from what I now call the Doing Disease. We've made productivity our religion and busyness our badge of honor. We wear exhaustion like a medal. We feel guilty for rest and suspicious of stillness.

I have a colleague whose sister lives in Germany. She described their cultural differences: after work, Germans gather with friends, turn grocery shopping into social events, build connection into daily routines. Americans, she said, come home in the middle of the night, buy groceries like a task to complete, fall into bed, and wake up to repeat the machine-like cycle.

We are machines. And machines break down.

The Doing Disease is a barrier because it convinces you that slowing down isn't an option. That your circumstances require this pace. That everyone operates this way, so it must be normal.

It's not normal. It's a cultural pathology, and it's killing us, through chronic stress, sleep deprivation, destroyed relationships, and lives that pass in a blur of tasks without meaning.

My grandfather used to say, "Stop and smell the roses." As a young person, I found this advice unbearably cheesy. Now I understand he was trying to teach me something urgent: that if you don't stop, life passes you by. You wake up at fifty-five wondering where the decades went, having accumulated achievements but missed the living that happens between them.

The Scarcity Trap

Part of what drives the Doing Disease is a deeper belief: that there isn't enough. Not enough time. Not enough money. Not enough security. Not enough of you to go around.

In America, this scarcity mindset is amplified by our lack of social safety nets. In Germany, if you lose your job, the government provides substantial support while you find your next opportunity. If you have a baby, you receive two years of paid leave. The safety net catches you, which allows you to take risks, to rest, to live with less constant anxiety.

Here, you're largely on your own. That reality breeds a particular kind of fear, the fear of what happens if something goes wrong, if the paycheck stops, if illness strikes, if the bottom falls out. We've all seen people for whom the bottom did fall out, and their fates haunt us.

I lived with this fear viscerally. My colleague shared her own story, how divorce left her starting from scratch, how those months of hardship burned a survival instinct into her psyche that never fully extinguished. "If I stop working," she told me, "I feel like I'll end up somewhere very bad. And I've seen what that looks like."

The scarcity trap keeps you running even when you've long since outpaced the danger. It's the voice that says "more" when you have enough. It's the impulse to hoard time, money, energy, to never let go, never relax, never trust that you're safe.

Breaking free requires recognizing when your fear is outdated, when you're responding to a threat that no longer exists, or that's far smaller than your nervous system believes.

Unrealistic Timelines: The Twenty-Year-Old With Three Jobs

I had a patient recently, a twenty-year-old, crying in my office, convinced she was a failure.

She had three jobs. She was sleeping four hours a night. She was stressed beyond her capacity. When I asked about her living situation, she told me she lived with her parents. No rent.

"So you have no housing costs," I said gently. "Why are you working three jobs?"

"I want to have my career where it needs to be. I want a car. I want everything set up."

"Your timeline isn't working for you," I told her. "You're trying to achieve in one year what takes a decade to build."

I watched the realization dawn on her face. She had absorbed a cultural message, probably from social media, that success should be immediate. That if she didn't have everything together by twenty-one, she was falling behind. That other people her age had figured it out, so why couldn't she?

This is another barrier: unrealistic expectations about how long meaningful change takes. We want transformation without process. Results without the slow work of building. We see the highlight reels of others' success and assume it happened overnight.

There's a Chinese proverb I love: "The journey of a thousand miles begins with a single step." Not a single leap. Not a single flight. A step. You have to walk before you can run.

When patients set goals, I encourage them to think in terms of seven days, seven months, seven years. The seven-day goals build momentum and prove that change is possible. The seven-month goals create visible transformation. The seven-year goals shape a life.

Most people abandon their efforts somewhere in the seven-day phase because they expected seven-year results immediately.

Toxic Environments: When the Barrier Is External

Not all barriers are internal. Sometimes the environment itself is the problem.

I see patients trapped in toxic workplaces, stressed and depressed, convinced they have no choice but to endure. They arrive with headaches, insomnia, weight gain, anxiety, all the physical manifestations of chronic stress. When I ask about their work, the floodgates open. A cruel supervisor. Unreasonable demands. A culture that punishes boundaries.

"I can't leave," they say. "I need this job."

Sometimes that's true in the immediate term. But often, "I can't leave" means "I'm afraid to leave." They've internalized the situation as permanent when it's actually changeable, with effort, planning, and courage.

I tell them directly: "This job is affecting your health. You have to make decisions." Health isn't negotiable. A paycheck means nothing if you're too sick, burned out, or broken to enjoy your life.

The same applies to relationships, living situations, and communities. If your environment consistently undermines your wellbeing, the barrier isn't inside you, it's around you. The breakthrough comes from changing your circumstances, not from adapting yourself to dysfunction.

I lived this with my own career. My early corporate medicine jobs were crushing me, the forced overtime, the fifteen-minute patient visits, the pressure to see more people faster. I blamed myself. I thought the problem was my inability to handle what every other doctor seemed to manage.

It took burnout, complete, devastating burnout, to show me that the environment was toxic. The breakthrough came when I stopped trying to survive within it and started designing something different: a four-day work week, clinics with cultures I chose, multiple income streams that gave me flexibility and choice.

What Burnout Teaches

When I gave my TEDx talk on physician burnout, I was speaking from raw experience. I had hit the wall. I was depleted in every dimension, physically exhausted, emotionally empty, questioning my entire career choice.

But here's what I've come to understand: burnout is a teacher. Not a pleasant one, I wouldn't wish it on anyone. But a teacher nonetheless.

In my deepest burnout, I asked myself a question that changed everything: "What is this burnout trying to teach me?"

The answer emerged slowly. It was teaching me that I had been living by default instead of design. I had taken jobs because they were available, not because they aligned with my values. I had accepted schedules that others imposed rather than creating ones that honored my wellbeing. I had prioritized external markers of success over internal experiences of fulfillment.

Burnout taught me my boundaries. It showed me what I could no longer tolerate. It forced me to ask what I actually wanted from my career, not what medical school implied I should want, not what colleagues seemed to accept, but what would allow me to practice medicine with joy rather than dread.

Some doctors leave medicine entirely when they burn out. They say, "Forget this, I'm done." I understand that choice. But I had invested thirteen years in becoming a physician, and I wanted to reclaim what had drawn me to medicine in the first place: the privilege of helping people heal.

The breakthrough came through intentional redesign. I didn't abandon my profession; I transformed my relationship with it.

Now I have career fulfillment. I'm thriving in my work rather than surviving it. The difference isn't that medicine changed, it's that I changed how I engage with it.

The Blessing of Crisis

At the University of Santa Monica, where I studied psychology, my professors taught a perspective that seemed counterintuitive at first: challenges are schools and sessions. They're not random misfortunes. They're curriculum.

I've seen this pattern repeatedly. Someone loses a loved one to a particular disease and becomes an advocate for research and prevention. Someone survives breast cancer and dedicates themselves to supporting other survivors. Someone experiences a tragedy that sparks a mission, a purpose, a reason to transform pain into contribution.

People need purpose. They need hope. And often, it's the difficult experiences, the barriers that seemed insurmountable, that forge the deepest sense of meaning.

I had a patient who grew up in the projects. Her mother was largely absent, caught in her own struggles. Every external factor predicted this woman would repeat the cycle. Instead, at seventeen, she left. She moved to a different city with nothing, no support, no resources, just determination. She worked, saved, put herself through law school. Today she's a successful attorney.

Her barriers could have defined her. Instead, they propelled her.

This doesn't mean every crisis is a blessing or that suffering should be romanticized. It means that within crisis, there's often a choice: let it crush you, or let it catalyze transformation.

Sitting With Yourself: Finding What's Missing

Breakthrough requires stillness. You can't identify your barriers while sprinting. You can't hear your inner wisdom over the noise of constant activity.

Everybody has to sit with themselves, become quiet, and ask: What makes me happy? What brings me fulfillment? What is missing?

That last question is crucial. Sometimes you feel dissatisfied without being able to pinpoint why. Something is off, but it's vague, amorphous. Until you can name what's missing, you can't address it.

Is it a relationship? A sense of purpose? Creative expression? Adventure? Rest? Community? Each person's answer is different.

For me, I discovered that I needed variety. Having one job with one employer created monotony and pressure. Now I have multiple roles, faculty at a medical school, urgent care shifts, my hospital panel, a private practice in wellness and weight loss. Each fulfills different needs. Together, they create richness.

I also discovered I needed novelty. Travel stimulates something in me, the freshness of new places, new cultures, new perspectives. When I went to Portugal, it wasn't just vacation. It was revelation. I came home knowing I wanted to integrate more of that European way of being into my American doing.

You have to find your own answers. They won't come from books or podcasts or other people's frameworks. They emerge from honest self-examination, from asking difficult questions and being willing to hear the answers.

From Default to Design

The greatest barrier of all is living by default.

Default means accepting whatever circumstances present themselves. Taking the job that's offered rather than seeking the job you want.

Staying in relationships because leaving seems too hard. Living where you've always lived because moving requires effort. Eating what's convenient instead of what nourishes. Filling time with screens because they're there.

Default feels easier in the moment. It requires no decision-making, no risk, no confrontation with your own desires. But default accumulates into a life you never chose, and one day you wake up wondering how you ended up here.

Design means intentionality. It means asking, "What do I actually want?" and then building toward that vision. It means recognizing that you have more choice than you think, even within constraints.

I defaulted into medicine in some ways, I knew I wanted healthcare, took the pre-nursing path, found myself with pre-med prerequisites, became a doctor. But I didn't design what kind of doctor I wanted to be or what my practice would look like. I just accepted what came next.

Burnout forced me to design. Now I'm intentional about my schedule, my clinic culture, my work-life boundaries. The difference in my wellbeing is immeasurable.

Social media shows you people living seemingly glamorous lives, and it's easy to feel jealous. But jealousy is a signal, it points toward what you want. Instead of resenting others' lives, use that feeling as data. What specifically appeals to you about what they have? Can you design elements of that into your own life?

At the beginning of each year, my family creates vision boards. We write goals across categories: career, health, wealth, relationships, travel, personal growth. We put these boards where we'll see them daily. And remarkably, many of those visions materialize.

This isn't magic. It's attention. When you articulate what you want, you begin noticing opportunities aligned with those desires. Your reticular activating system, the part of your brain that filters information, starts flagging relevant possibilities. You make different choices because you're oriented toward a destination rather than drifting.

The Breakthrough Formula

After years of helping patients break through their barriers, I've identified a simple formula:

Awareness + Acceptance + Action = Breakthrough

Awareness means seeing your barriers clearly. Not the stories you tell about them, but the actual obstacles, the fears, beliefs, environments, and patterns that hold you back. This requires honesty, often uncomfortable honesty.

Acceptance means acknowledging reality without judgment. Yes, you carry childhood wounds around money. Yes, you've been living by default. Yes, your job is toxic. Yes, your timeline is unrealistic. Acceptance isn't approval, it's simply seeing what is, clearly, so you can work with it.

Action means taking concrete steps, even small ones. Awareness and acceptance without action leave you stuck in contemplation. You understand your barriers but don't move past them. Action breaks the paralysis.

Some people get stuck at awareness, they see the problem but can't accept it. Some accept the problem but take no action. Complete breakthrough requires all three.

Healing, Hope, Faith

The journey through barriers follows a particular arc: healing leads to hope, and hope enables faith.

Healing comes first. You cannot build a thriving life on a foundation of unaddressed wounds. The childhood scarcity that drives you. The relationship trauma that makes you guarded. The professional failure that shattered your confidence. The loss that left you grieving. These wounds need attention, through therapy, through reflection, through whatever practices help you process and integrate painful experiences.

As you heal, **hope** emerges. You begin to believe that things can be different. Not naive optimism that ignores reality, but grounded hope based on evidence, small changes that proved possible, glimpses of what life could feel like.

And hope cultivates **faith**, trust in yourself, in the process, in the unfolding of your life. Faith that if you take the next step, the path will continue to reveal itself. Faith that you're capable of creating the life you envision.

This isn't necessarily religious faith, though it can be. It's faith in possibility. Faith that your efforts matter. Faith that design works better than default.

It's Hard to Be Heavy. It's Hard to Be Fit. Choose Your Hard.

I share this phrase with patients often: It's hard to be heavy. It's hard to be fit. Choose your hard.

Both paths involve difficulty. Carrying excess weight is hard, on your joints, your heart, your self-image, your mobility. But getting fit is also hard, the discipline, the discomfort, the consistency required.

The same logic applies to every dimension of life. It's hard to stay in a soul-crushing job. It's hard to search for a new one. Choose your hard. It's hard to remain in an unfulfilling relationship. It's hard to be alone while seeking something better. Choose your hard.

The point isn't that one path is easy. Nothing worth having comes without effort. The point is that you get to choose which difficulty you embrace. One leads toward the life you want; the other keeps you stuck.

Breakthroughs require work. There's no shortcut, no hack, no way to bypass the process. The patients who yo-yo, losing weight and regaining it, starting and stopping, making progress and sliding back, are usually the ones looking for overnight success.

Sustainable transformation comes from consistent small actions, repeated over time, until they become who you are.

Your Barrier Inventory

Before moving to the practical work of the next chapter, I want you to take an honest inventory. What barriers stand between you and the life you're designing?

Consider each category:

Fear-Based Barriers: What are you afraid of? Financial insecurity? Failure? Success? Judgment? Being alone? Name your fears specifically.

Belief-Based Barriers: What do you believe about yourself or the world that might be limiting? "I'm not disciplined enough." "People like me don't succeed." "It's too late to change." Identify the stories you tell.

Environmental Barriers: What in your surroundings works against your goals? A toxic workplace? Unsupportive relationships? A neighborhood without walkable streets? An environment that makes healthy eating difficult?

Habit-Based Barriers: What automatic behaviors undermine your intentions? The phone-checking that steals your mornings? The stress-eating that follows hard days? The procrastination that delays important changes?

Timeline Barriers: Are your expectations realistic? Are you trying to achieve in months what requires years? Are you abandoning efforts too quickly because results don't appear fast enough?

Write down what comes up. Be specific. The clearer you can name your barriers, the more effectively you can address them.

And remember: barriers aren't character flaws. They're obstacles. Obstacles can be navigated, climbed over, worked around, or removed. But only if you see them first.

The Breakthrough Waiting for You

On the other side of your barriers is a life you can barely imagine from where you stand now. Not a perfect life, perfection doesn't exist. But a designed life. An intentional life. A life where you thrive rather than merely survive.

I think of the patient who arrived burned out, certain she couldn't leave her toxic job. She identified her barriers, fear of financial instability, beliefs about what "responsible" adults do, an environment that normalized dysfunction. She did the work of awareness, acceptance, and action. Two years later, she runs her own practice on her own terms, healthier and happier than she ever was in corporate medicine.

I think of my own journey from burnout to fulfillment. From default to design. From a schedule that crushed me to one that sustains me.

Your breakthrough is waiting. It might come through gradual evolution or sudden realization. It might require professional help or simply honest self-reflection. It might be easy in some dimensions and brutally difficult in others.

But it's possible. That's what I want you to hold onto as we move into the practical work ahead.

Your barriers are real. And they're not permanent.

In the next chapter, we'll transform everything we've discussed throughout this book into concrete action, a seven-day kickstart to build momentum, followed by a thirty-day challenge to create lasting change. It's time to stop reading about the designed life and start living it.

Reflection Questions for Chapter 7

1. What is your deepest fear about making significant changes in your life? Where does that fear originate?
2. Do you suffer from the "Doing Disease"? How much of your identity is tied to productivity and busyness?
3. What scarcity beliefs do you carry, about time, money, opportunity, or worthiness? Are these beliefs still accurate, or are they outdated?
4. Are your timelines for change realistic? Are you expecting overnight transformation when the work requires months or years?
5. Is your environment supporting or undermining your goals? What would need to change?
6. If your current challenges are "schools and sessions," what might they be trying to teach you?
7. Where in your life are you living by default rather than design? What would intentional choice look like?
8. Consider the formula: Awareness + Acceptance + Action = Breakthrough. Where do you tend to get stuck?

Chapter 7 Action Items

This Week

- ❑ Complete a barrier inventory: write down your fear-based, belief-based, environmental, habit-based, and timeline barriers
- ❑ Identify one area where you're living by default and envision what design would look like
- ❑ Schedule thirty minutes of stillness, no phone, no tasks, just sitting with yourself
- ❑ Ask yourself: "What is missing?" Write whatever comes up without judgment

This Month

- ❑ Create a vision board for the upcoming year with specific categories: health, career, relationships, finances, personal growth, and experiences
- ❑ Choose one fear to confront and take one small action toward it
- ❑ If your environment is toxic, develop an exit plan, even if you're not ready to execute it immediately
- ❑ Introduce one practice of "being" into your "doing" life: a slow meal, an unscheduled afternoon, time in nature without agenda

This Quarter

- ❑ Address one limiting belief through therapy, coaching, or deliberate mindset work

- ❑ Make one significant environmental change that removes barriers to your goals
- ❑ Establish one practice of regular self-reflection: journaling, meditation, or intentional conversation with a trusted friend
- ❑ Evaluate progress with compassion, noting breakthroughs without judging yourself for remaining barriers

Start Today

Name one barrier out loud. Just one. Say it to yourself, write it down, or share it with someone you trust. The barrier that remains hidden retains its power. The barrier you name begins to lose its grip.

Name it. That's your first breakthrough.

Chapter 8: The 7-Day Kitchen Start + 30-Day Challenge

"Just start."

Start Something. Start Anything. Start Now.

You've read the book. You understand the principles. You know about presence and intention, nutrition and movement, community and career, authentic self and barriers to breakthrough.

Now what?

This is where most people stall. They absorb information without transforming it into action. They highlight passages, make mental notes, feel inspired, and then return to the same patterns that brought them to the book in the first place.

That's not going to be you.

When I was starting my private practice in wellness and weight loss, someone gave me advice that changed everything: "Just start. Open the doors. You may not be fully ready. You may make mistakes. But you have to start to see that first patient."

That wisdom applies to everything in life. Career switches. Health transformations. Relationship changes. Creative projects. The beginning is always the hardest part, not because the work is hardest there, but because inertia is strongest.

This chapter is your kickstart. We're going to take the principles from throughout this book and transform them into a practical, day-by-day program. First, a seven-day intensive to build momentum and prove to yourself that change is possible. Then, a thirty-day challenge to deepen those changes into habits that stick.

You've picked up this book because something in your life wasn't working. You've stayed with it because you want something different. Now it's time to create that something different, not in theory, but in the actual fabric of your daily life.

Let's begin.

The Philosophy Behind the Challenge

Before we dive into the specific days, I want you to understand the principles guiding this program.

Start small and build momentum. We're not overhauling your entire life in one day. Dramatic transformations rarely last. Instead, we're introducing one focused change at a time, allowing each to settle before adding the next. By the end of seven days, you'll have established foundations across multiple dimensions. By the end of thirty days, those foundations will feel like second nature.

Progress, not perfection. You will not execute this program perfectly. Some days you'll hit every target; other days life will intervene. That's fine. What matters is returning to the path after you stumble, not walking it flawlessly. Perfectionists fail because the first mistake derails them entirely. Progress-minded people fail, learn, adjust, and continue.

Intentions create direction. Each day begins with setting an intention. This isn't empty ritual, it's programming your mind for what matters. When you declare what you're focused on, you prime your attention to notice relevant opportunities and your will to resist irrelevant distractions.

Reflection cements learning. Each day ends with reflection. What worked? What didn't? What did you notice? Without reflection, experiences pass without teaching. With reflection, every day becomes data for improvement.

The goal is thriving, not surviving. You're not just trying to get through the day, pay the bills, check the boxes. You're designing a life of purpose, connection, vitality, and joy. Keep that vision at the forefront as you work through each challenge.

The 7-Day Kickstart

These seven days are designed to touch every major dimension we've covered in this book. Each day has a theme, specific actions, and space for reflection. Complete them in order, as each builds on the previous.

Day 1: Intention Setting

Theme: Establishing your foundation

Today is about clarity. Before you change anything external, you need to articulate what you're changing toward.

Morning Practice: Before reaching for your phone, sit quietly for five minutes. Take deep breaths. Ask yourself: What do I want my life to look like? What would thriving feel like? Don't censor or judge, just let answers arise.

Day's Assignment: Write your Life Design Intention. This is a paragraph or page describing the life you're working toward. Include how you want to feel in your body. How you want your relationships to feel. What your work life looks like. How you spend your time. Be specific and write in present tense, as if it's already true: "I wake up feeling energized. I nourish my body with whole foods. I have meaningful work that challenges and fulfills me."

Evening Reflection: Read your intention aloud. How does it feel to declare this vision? What emotions arise, excitement, doubt, longing? Write a few sentences about the experience.

Day 2: Sleep Reset

Theme: Building from rest

Sleep is the foundation of everything else. Without adequate rest, your willpower depletes, your food cravings intensify, your stress resilience crumbles, and your clarity fades. We start with sleep because it multiplies the effectiveness of every other change.

Morning Practice: Note how you feel upon waking. Are you groggy or refreshed? Did you sleep through the night? What time did you actually get to bed? This is your baseline.

Day's Assignment: Establish your sleep architecture. Calculate what time you need to be asleep to get seven hours before your wake time.

Then calculate when to start your wind-down routine, ideally sixty to ninety minutes before sleep. This evening, put the plan into action: screens off at your designated time, wind-down routine engaged, lights out at your target.

Create a sleep sanctuary if you haven't: cool temperature, complete darkness, phone charging outside the bedroom or at minimum on do-not-disturb mode.

Evening Reflection: Before beginning your wind-down, write tomorrow's intention: to wake after seven hours of quality sleep feeling more rested than today.

Day 3: Nutrition Swap

Theme: One change on your plate

We're not overhauling your diet today. We're making one strategic swap that will ripple through your nutrition. Remember: the anti-inflammatory diet isn't about restriction, it's about choosing foods that heal rather than harm.

Morning Practice: Drink a full glass of water before consuming anything else. Calculate your daily water target (body weight divided by two, in ounces). Set reminders if needed to hit this target throughout the day.

Day's Assignment: Choose your swap. Options include:

- Replace one sugary drink with water or green tea
- Add vegetables to one meal that typically lacks them
- Swap white rice or pasta for a whole grain alternative

• Replace a processed snack with nuts, fruit, or vegetables with hummus

• Cook one meal at home that you'd typically order out

Execute this swap today. Notice how it feels, physically and emotionally.

Evening Reflection: How was the swap? Difficult or easy? What would help you sustain it? Write a sentence committing to continue this swap for the remainder of the challenge.

Day 4: Movement Baseline

Theme: Getting your body moving

Motion is lotion. Today we establish that exercise isn't about punishment or perfection, it's about honoring your body's design to move.

Morning Practice: Before anything else, do five minutes of stretching. Nothing elaborate, just gentle movements to wake your body. Notice areas of tightness.

Day's Assignment: Complete thirty minutes of cardiovascular movement. This can be:

• A brisk walk (outdoors is ideal for the bonus of nature and vitamin D)

• A jog or run

• A dance session in your living room

• A gym class or home workout video

• Swimming, cycling, or any activity that elevates your heart rate

The goal is to breathe hard enough that conversation would be difficult but not impossible. If thirty continuous minutes feels daunting, break it into three ten-minute sessions.

Evening Reflection: How do you feel after moving? More energized or tired? What form of movement did you enjoy most? What time of day worked best? Record these insights, they'll guide your ongoing exercise routine.

Day 5: Connection Outreach

Theme: Reaching toward community

Humans are wired for connection. Loneliness is as dangerous to health as smoking. Today we prioritize relationship, not the passive connection of social media, but active, intentional reaching out.

Morning Practice: Think of three people who matter to you. Visualize their faces. Feel gratitude for their presence in your life.

Day's Assignment: Make meaningful contact with at least one person. Not a quick text. Not a social media like. Real connection:

• Call someone and have an actual conversation

• Meet a friend for coffee or a meal

• Write a heartfelt message telling someone what they mean to you

• Schedule a future gathering, a date night, a dinner party, a walk with a friend

If you're partnered, this is a good day to prioritize that relationship. Put phones away. Have a conversation without distraction. Remember why you chose each other.

Evening Reflection: How did connection feel? Did you resist reaching out? What made it easier or harder? Do you feel more energized after human contact, or does it drain you? Both reactions tell you something important about your needs.

Day 6: Play and Joy

Theme: Remembering what makes you come alive

When was the last time you did something purely for fun? Not productive, not obligatory, not valuable for any reason except that it brings you joy? Adults often forget how to play. Today we remember.

Morning Practice: List five activities that brought you joy as a child or young adult. Did you love drawing? Playing sports? Reading for hours? Dancing? Building things? Making music? Let yourself remember.

Day's Assignment: Dedicate at least one hour to play. This is non-negotiable and non-productive time. Options include:

- A hobby you've neglected (painting, music, gardening, crafts)
- Unstructured time in nature, no destination, just wandering
- A game, board game, card game, video game, sport
- Dancing to your favorite music
- Playing with children or pets

• Reading fiction purely for pleasure

• Cooking an elaborate meal as a creative act, not a chore

The only rule: this time cannot be about accomplishment. It's about enjoyment.

Evening Reflection: What did you choose? How did it feel to give yourself permission to play? Did guilt arise? Did time pass quickly or slowly? What does this experience teach you about what's missing in your regular life?

Day 7: Reflect and Commit

Theme: Integration and forward motion

You've completed six days of intentional living. Today we integrate what you've learned and commit to continuing.

Morning Practice: Read your Day 1 Life Design Intention aloud. How does it feel now, after six days of action? More possible? More urgent? More specific?

Day's Assignment: Complete a full review and commitment:

Review: For each of the past six days, write one sentence about what you learned or experienced:

• Day 1 (Intention): What clarity emerged?

• Day 2 (Sleep): How did prioritizing rest affect you?

• Day 3 (Nutrition): What did your food swap teach you?

• Day 4 (Movement): How did your body respond to exercise?

• Day 5 (Connection): What happened when you reached out?

• Day 6 (Play): What did you rediscover about joy?

Commit: Decide which practices you'll carry forward into the 30-Day Challenge. Write a statement of commitment. Sign and date it. This is your contract with yourself.

Evening Reflection: You've just proven that change is possible. In one week, you've touched sleep, nutrition, movement, connection, and joy. You've set intentions and reflected on outcomes. This is the template for designed living. Tomorrow, you expand it.

The 30-Day Challenge

The kickstart created momentum. The thirty-day challenge transforms momentum into habit.

Research suggests that habits take an average of sixty-six days to become automatic, though the range varies widely. Thirty days won't complete the habit-formation process, but it will establish patterns firmly enough that continuing feels natural rather than forced.

Here's how the next thirty days work:

Daily Non-Negotiables

Every day of the challenge, you maintain these five practices:

1. Morning Intention (5 minutes): Before checking your phone, take five minutes for intention-setting. This can be meditation, gratitude practice, or simply sitting quietly and asking, "What matters today?"

2. Hydration Target: Drink your calculated water intake (body weight divided by two, in ounces). Track this if helpful.

3. Movement Minimum: At minimum, ten minutes of intentional movement daily. Aim for thirty minutes five days per week, but never zero.

4. Sleep Protection: Honor your sleep architecture. Wind-down begins at your designated time. Seven hours minimum in bed.

5. Evening Reflection (5 minutes): Before bed, review your day. What worked? What didn't? What will you carry forward?

Weekly Focuses

In addition to daily non-negotiables, each week has a particular focus:

Week 1 (Days 8-14): Nutrition Foundation

- Continue your Day 3 swap and add one additional nutrition improvement
- Plan and shop for healthy meals on Sunday
- Cook at home at least four times this week
- Begin a simple food log, not calories, just what you eat and how you feel afterward
- Try one new anti-inflammatory recipe

Week 2 (Days 15-21): Movement Expansion

- Increase to thirty minutes of cardiovascular exercise five times
- Add two strength training sessions (bodyweight exercises count)

- Establish your optimal exercise time and protect it on your calendar
- Try one new form of movement, a class, a sport, a different route
- Find an accountability partner for exercise

Week 3 (Days 22-28): Connection and Community

- Reach out to at least one person daily, text, call, or in-person
- Schedule a date night or quality time with your partner (if applicable)
- Attend one group activity, class, club, community event, or religious service
- Limit social media to thirty minutes daily; notice how this affects your mood
- Identify one relationship that needs attention and take a step toward nurturing it

Week 4 (Days 29-37): Integration and Design

- Review your Life Design Intention, revise based on what you've learned
- Create or update your vision board
- Conduct a career checkup, are you fulfilled, compensated fairly, in a healthy environment?
- Review your finances against the 50-30-20 framework
- Identify remaining barriers and create a plan for addressing them

• Schedule your next thirty days, insert joy, rest, connection, and movement

KonMari Your Schedule

Throughout this challenge, I want you to apply the KonMari principle to your time. Marie Kondo asks about possessions: "Does this spark joy?" Ask the same of your calendar.

Your schedule should be filled with things that bring you purpose, connection, growth, or genuine satisfaction. Obligations that drain you without returning value need examination. Are they truly necessary? Can they be delegated, reduced, or eliminated?

This doesn't mean every moment will be joyful, life includes mundane tasks and difficult responsibilities. But the overall balance of your time should trend toward thriving rather than merely surviving.

During Week 4, you'll review your schedule with this lens. What's working? What's not? What would you eliminate if you could? What would you add if you made space?

Tracking Your Progress

Create a simple tracking system for the thirty days. This can be a journal, a checklist, or an app, whatever you'll actually use. Each day, record:

• Hours of sleep

• Minutes of movement

- Water intake
- Notable nutrition choices (positive or negative)
- Connection made
- Mood (1-10 scale)
- Energy level (1-10 scale)
- One thing you're grateful for

Over thirty days, this data reveals patterns. You'll see which practices most improve your mood, which factors disrupt your sleep, which connections energize you. This information is gold for designing the rest of your life.

When You Stumble

You will have imperfect days. Maybe several of them. Here's what matters: when you stumble, you don't stop.

Miss your morning intention? Do it at noon. Skip exercise? Walk for ten minutes before bed. Eat something that doesn't serve you? Make the next meal nourishing. Have a day where everything falls apart? Wake up tomorrow and begin again.

Progress isn't linear. It's not about perfect adherence, it's about overall trajectory. If you complete the thirty days with 80% consistency, you've transformed your baseline. Even 60% consistency means you've practiced these habits more than you would have otherwise.

The voice that says "you've already failed, might as well quit" is lying. Every moment is a fresh opportunity to choose differently.

After the Challenge

Day 37 arrives. What happens next?

Ideally, these practices have become automatic enough that continuing doesn't require the structured challenge format. The morning intention is just what you do. The water intake is habit. The movement is non-negotiable. The evening reflection is routine.

But you might need structure longer, and that's okay. You could:

• Repeat the 30-Day Challenge with the same or modified focus

• Create your own challenge based on remaining barriers

• Join a community, running group, meal prep club, accountability partnership

• Work with a coach, trainer, or therapist to address specific areas

The point isn't that Day 37 marks completion. The point is that you've proven to yourself what's possible and established a foundation for lifelong growth.

Your Designed Life Awaits

Throughout this book, we've explored what it means to thrive, not merely survive. We've looked at presence and intention, nutrition and movement, rest and renewal, community and connection, career and finances, authentic self and barriers to breakthrough.

Now you have a roadmap.

The seven-day kickstart proves that change is possible. The thirty-day challenge transforms possibility into practice. And the principles you've learned will guide you far beyond these pages.

Remember: life happens in the small choices. The decision to wake up with intention rather than reaching immediately for your phone. The choice to nourish rather than merely fill. The commitment to move your body even when motivation is low. The courage to reach out, to play, to rest, to design rather than default.

You're not becoming someone new. You're becoming more fully yourself, the self that was always possible, waiting beneath the accumulated habits and fears and defaults.

That self is ready to emerge.

Start today. Start now. Just start.

Your designed life is waiting.

Reflection Questions for Chapter 8

1. What is your immediate reaction to this structured program? Excitement? Overwhelm? Skepticism? Acknowledge the reaction without judging it.
2. Which of the seven kickstart days feels most challenging? Which feels most appealing? What does this tell you about where you need growth?
3. What has stopped you from implementing similar changes in the past? How will you address those obstacles this time?
4. Who in your life could support you through this challenge? Who might inadvertently undermine it?
5. If you completed this program successfully, how would your life be different in thirty-seven days? Visualize it specifically.
6. What will you do when you stumble, because you will? Write your plan for returning to the path.
7. Beyond this challenge, what does your designed life look like in one year? Five years? Ten years?
8. What would it mean to you to stop surviving and start thriving?

Chapter 8 Action Items

Before You Begin

- ❑ Choose your start date, ideally within the next three days
- ❑ Gather supplies: a journal or notebook for tracking and reflection, healthy foods for your kitchen, comfortable clothes for exercise
- ❑ Clear your calendar of non-essential commitments for Day 1

- [ ] Inform someone you trust that you're starting this challenge, accountability increases success

During the 7-Day Kickstart

- [ ] Complete each day's specific assignment
- [ ] Write in your journal every morning and evening
- [ ] Don't skip ahead, trust the process and take each day as it comes
- [ ] If you miss a day, simply do it the next day, don't abandon the process

During the 30-Day Challenge

- [ ] Maintain the five daily non-negotiables
- [ ] Focus on each week's specific theme while sustaining previous weeks' gains
- [ ] Track your progress daily
- [ ] Review at the end of each week: What's working? What needs adjustment?
- [ ] Practice self-compassion, this is about progress, not perfection

After Day 37

- [ ] Conduct a comprehensive review: Which practices will you maintain? Which need modification?
- [ ] Update your Life Design Intention based on what you've learned

- ❑ Decide your next phase, repeat, modify, or graduate to maintenance mode
- ❑ Celebrate your accomplishment, you've done something significant

Start Today

Right now, before you close this book:

Choose your Day 1. Write it down. Tell someone.

That's it. That's your first step on the journey of a thousand miles.

The designed life doesn't build itself. It requires your intention, your action, your consistency, your courage.

You have everything you need.

Now go live it.

The End

www.ingramcontent.com/pod-product-compliance
Lightning Source LLC
LaVergne TN
LVHW022218200926
848481LV00006B/2023